the POWER of Your SPIRIT

ALSO BY SONIA CHOQUETTE

AUDIO PROGRAMS

All of the above are available at your
local bookstore, or may be ordered by visiting:

Hay House USA: **www.hayhouse.com**®
Hay House Australia: **www.hayhouse.com.au**
Hay House UK: **www.hayhouse.co.uk**
Hay House India: **www.hayhouse.co.in**

the POWER
of Your
SPIRIT

A GUIDE TO JOYFUL LIVING

SONIA CHOQUETTE

HAY HOUSE, INC.
Carlsbad, California • New York City
London • Sydney • New Delhi

Published in the United States by: Hay House, Inc.: www.hayhouse.
com • **Published in Australia by:** Hay House Australia Pty. Ltd.: www.
hayhouse.com.au • **Published in the United Kingdom by:** Hay House
UK, Ltd.: www.hayhouse.co.uk • **Published in India by:** Hay House
Publishers India: www.hayhouse.co.in

Editorial supervision: Jill Kramer • *Project editor:* Lisa Mitchell
Cover design: Christy Salinas • *Interior design:* Tricia Breidenthal

The Rumi quotation in Chapter 5 was used by permission of the translator, Coleman Barks.

Library of Congress Cataloging-in-Publication Data

Choquette, Sonia.
 The power of your spirit : a guide to joyful living / Sonia Choquette.
  p. cm.
 ISBN 978-1-4019-2809-4 (hardcover : alk. paper) 1. Parapsychology.
2. Spiritual life--Miscellanea. I. Title.
 BF1031.C517 2011
 133.9--dc22
                                                 2010049777

Tradepaper ISBN: 978-1-4019-7810-5
E-book ISBN: 978-1-4019-3097-4

1st edition, May 2011
2nd edition, June 2012

Printed in the United States of America

This product uses papers sourced from responsibly managed forests.
For more information, see www.hayhouse.com.

*To the Holy Spirit, the Divine Source
of All Life. I offer this book in humble
service to, and in deepest gratitude for,
your never-ending loving light upon us all.
Thank you for the gift of my life.*

CONTENTS

INTRODUCTION

"Pure logic is the ruin of the spirit."
— ANTOINE DE SAINT-EXUPÉRY

Several months ago, I found myself in a hotel room in San Diego after presenting an all-day workshop to several hundred people. Tired and ready to relax, I decided to order room service and rent a movie. After skimming through the selections for something light and funny, I finally settled on a romantic comedy called *My Life in Ruins*.

The movie itself was cute enough, but the main character's struggle actually made a big impression on me. Georgia, a young Greek-American tour guide living in Greece, is unhappy and frustrated with life. Her friends tell her it's because she has lost her *kefi*, a Greek word for "Spirit." To them, this was the obvious reason for her misery and why nothing in her life seemed to work out. To make matters worse, no person or event could change her situation. It was up to Georgia to rediscover her magic power, her kefi. Otherwise, her world would remain colorless, uninspiring . . . and most likely, loveless. Only she could uncover her inner spark and get back into the flow of life.

Like most Hollywood stories, this one has a happy ending. Georgia reconnects with her Spirit; and she finds that her life once again has profound meaning, laughter, and love. That night I went to sleep feeling happy and relieved. One more person who found her Spirit—even if only in the movies—meant one less miserable person in the world. Hooray!

The film reminded me that the idea of losing your connection to Spirit isn't that unusual. In fact, it might be the most common problem from which people suffer today. In my 35 years of experience as a professional intuitive counselor and teacher, I've come across this quite often. Through my one-on-one intuitive sessions and the classes I teach, I work intimately with thousands of men and women all over the world. I continually encounter incredibly lovely, generous, and caring individuals who feel lost, disillusioned, and powerless. Yet most of them also know in their hearts that there must be another way to live.

Reconnecting with Your Divine Self

We all want to successfully deal with challenges, face disappointment with grace, tap into our inner power and creative expression, feel excited by a purpose, and live by an intuitive guiding wisdom. We want to be more spontaneous and carefree—laughing or singing out loud, and dancing with abandon. We want to open our hearts, leave our fears behind, and find genuine peace no matter what is happening around us. To put it simply, like Georgia, we want to reclaim our kefi and get our Spirit back.

But as much as we wish for a significant spiritual breakthrough, as much as we long to know our Divine self and uncover our intuitive genius, we're still not making the commitment that will ensure our success. We want the gifts, but we aren't engaging in the practical work necessary to obtain them . . . so we remain stuck—and more discouraged than ever. When it comes to being empowered, we're like window-shoppers on Madison Avenue, gazing longingly at the incredible possibilities dangling before our eyes, yet not claiming them as our own.

I believe the reason for this frustration and spiritual impasse is that way too many of us are trying to make a transformational, energetic shift through intellectual means alone. We make the mistake of thinking that knowing something is the equivalent of integrating and embodying this wisdom into our being. In other words, we *know* a lot about the power of Spirit, but we aren't actually *experiencing* it. And we can't do so through intellectual pursuits alone. In fact, we cannot experience the power of Spirit through the intellect (or ego) at all. It is only achievable through a deep, intentional daily practice of connecting with Spirit.

This is the most authentic, lasting power we have in our lives. We can't control the outside world, but with the power of Spirit, we *can* create a sense of purpose within that brings about deep satisfaction and personal peace—regardless of what is going on around us.

We can't be truly happy without making this connection and surrendering to our Spirit. Otherwise, it's
like being lost in the jungle with no clear path, no ori-
entation . . . no clue as to how to find our way home.
This state of mind is quite similar to the stress, fear, and
exhaustion so many of us feel on a daily basis.

We have become submissive, duality-based, ego-
identified victims. We've been conditioned to, and even
forced into, handing our power over to others—only
for it to be used against us. We've been misguided or
misdirected in almost every imaginable way, and we've
accepted and woven this belief system into our cellular
bodies and even our DNA. We've been trained to think
that we are something other than what we really are;
and instead of using our Divinely appointed, creative
spiritual powers, we believe what we have been told: that
we are unlovable, unworthy, and even, at times, unwanted. We've convinced ourselves that we're tainted, broken
beings who must submit to others in order to feel love or
achieve success.

The perpetual stress and internal chaos of a life
without the power of Spirit causes innumerable physical
and psychological breakdowns, and even accidents. The
more I think about it, the more I am convinced that the
loss of Spirit is the root cause for most depression, addiction, disease, and discontent. But the worst consequence
of a life disconnected from Spirit is that we lose touch
with our deepest sense of personal creativity, which is
the spark of Spirit in action.

A life without genuine creative expression lacks
meaning and purpose. People in this state tend to find
negative ways to distract themselves and deaden the
emptiness they feel. Whether this leads to destructive

behaviors or emotions, frequent accidents or illnesses, career stalls or chronic unemployment, or outbursts of rage or social withdrawal, soon the problem becomes others' problems as well. All paths are interwoven—we are connected to one another, and one person's misery eventually affects everyone else. Therefore, not only is our connection to Spirit an essential personal need, it's also a profoundly important familial and social need.

Pursuing your Spirit over ego provides a deep-seated, unwavering sense of protection and safety. It relaxes your mind, puts your body at ease, and opens your heart. A connection to Spirit restores your confidence, relieves your anxiety, and frees you from the desire to control everything in your life. With such a big load off your shoulders, you can actually begin to sense your intuition (the voice of your Spirit), which is extremely subtle at first—and when you're under a lot of stress, it's easily missed. With intuition firmly at the helm of your life, you reconnect with the deepest, most authentic truth of your being and remember who you are as God designed and created you to be: perfect, beautiful, and whole.

With Spirit as your guide, you don't have to base your identify or self-worth on how people view you. Because you know who you are, you're free to be yourself and can experience others as they are as well; you no longer need to get anyone else's approval.

Such authentic self-awareness encourages the same transformation in others when they're in your presence. Everyone you interact with energetically senses your genuineness, so the typical manipulations people engage in to feel safe and win approval cease, and more heart-to-heart connections take their place. You no longer feel the need to struggle with others for power because your power arises from within, so bit by bit you unlearn entrenched patterns and behaviors of conflict. Guided by your Spirit, you experience a heightened awareness that allows you to see individuals with greater compassion and clarity. You begin to understand their fear as a symptom of having lost their Spirit, so you no longer take their unconscious negative behaviors personally. With Spirit in your heart, the dark, heavy cloud of defense and suspicion lifts. You go through life with fewer filters, and it becomes brighter and more beautiful than ever before.

Reaching for this book on a shelf or having it come into your possession in some other way is a strong indication that, on a soul level, your desire to connect with the power of your Spirit is now being felt. This is an exciting turning point for you because not only are you in search of your Spirit, but your Spirit is also in search of *you*. It is calling you back to your true power. You need it, and the world needs it from you.

The Road Ahead

The return to your authentic self isn't easy, however. Throughout this journey, you will be challenged again and again to face your fears and embrace your truths. Although difficult, it's a transformational experience that you're invited to take simply by virtue of incarnating as a Divine being in this grand human experiment.

The process unfolds in four distinct stages, each one propelling you to the next. How fast or slow you move through them depends on your desire, courage, and willpower. It's important to keep in mind, though, that this soul journey is individual and organic; you must move along at your own pace. It's not a contest. Rather, like most profound experiences, the "getting there" part provides you with the best opportunities for healing and positive change. Sooner or later, all of us will come full circle . . . whether in this lifetime or the next.

The key to your success is to earnestly begin the process of unlearning and undoing the false, limited habits and beliefs of the inauthentic self that have imprisoned you, and replacing them with the liberating, conscious habits of a Divine creator. You have to be disciplined and commit yourself to practicing daily until Divinely conscious habits become second nature—and ultimately, the only way you choose to live.

Walking away from lifetimes of falsely constructed, deeply wounded, and victimized ego identification and fully embodying the expansive expression of your authentic, unlimited, multidimensional Holy Self is a courageous, step-by-step process. Your shift from one to the other doesn't happen automatically. It will come about only as a result of your intense desire and conscious choice to grow into your truth on a daily basis.

So when you really feel like you're ready to reclaim *your* kefi—to fully realize the power of your Spirit—turn the page . . . and let the transformation begin!

HOW TO USE THIS BOOK

I offer this book as an accessible, practical guide to help you return to personal empowerment. There are four stages you must pass through on the way to reconnecting with your Spirit: *Awakening, Discovery, Surrender,* and *Flow.* As you enter each stage of soul evolution, it leads you farther away from the trance and traps of your limited ego perceptions, and closer to your true spiritual nature. Although it's possible to move through all four stages in one dramatic shift, this is a rare exception.

For most of us, the journey from our limited ego perception to the unlimited, higher awareness of our Divine nature is gradual. We set the pace from within, motivated by our own volition, and our desire to connect with our authentic self.

Included within these chapters are many sets of questions for you to ponder and explore. They will help you make direct contact with your Spirit, for only your Spirit can answer honestly. Following the questions, I've also added several simple daily practices to help you embrace what you've learned so that this new awareness of your Spirit feels natural and easy. These steps are clearly laid out to allow you to make the shift without getting off track or backtracking to the dead end of victimhood.

Be patient with yourself as you return to Spirit. It may seem elusive, but one day—and it may be sooner than you think—everything will suddenly just click; and you'll find yourself in an unconditionally loving, unlimited flow with your Spirit. If you have the intention to become more and more aware of your genuine self and also do the daily work, the Universe will oversee the big stuff.

The biggest step toward freeing the power of Spirit within comes from being more and more authentic with yourself and others. Doing so isn't necessarily an easy or clear assignment, especially for those who have been trained to hide or ignore their feelings all their lives. A good way to discover your true self is to write about how you feel on a regular basis. Therefore, while working through the stages in this book, I strongly suggest that you keep a journal and also use it to answer the questions within the chapters. Go deep within and find your genuine response. Keep in mind that the intellect likes to rush through things rather than be present. This book is designed to free you from the need to always have to get somewhere or be someone you aren't.

Take your time and enjoy the process. Ponder the questions and stories throughout. Be sure to implement at least one of the daily practices on a regular basis for at least 40 days. This is necessary because in order to effectively shift your vibration (and *live in* the flow and power of Spirit), you must change the frequency at which you normally vibrate, and this takes at least 40 days to accomplish.

◎ ◎

There's just one more thing I want to share before we begin. I'm writing this book as much for myself (or at least my "ego-self") as for you. I, too, am learning and growing as I continue to surrender my ego, and it is my authentic Spirit writing through me that has filled these pages . . . so I've been especially interested in what has come through!

We are all in various stages of living in a higher, more expanded state of consciousness during these transformational times. We are all students. Each story I share in this book is my own, or comes by way of my clients and friends, and is intended to honestly reflect the challenges we face in learning to flow as Divine beings in Spirit. We all have a piece to contribute to the great puzzle of transformation, because there is only one Spirit in which we all live, breathe, and exist. As we each effect positive change as individuals, at the same time we're helping others find their way home, too.

It is my sincere wish and prayer that we all experience a grounded, guided journey from ego to the power of Spirit. May we feel the presence of Spirit within, and remember and witness the Holy Spirit in each other, knowing that we are all returning to our true and holy nature. And may we resist the urge to turn back in fear or fantasy to victimhood, however tempting it may be in the moment.

Author's note: All of the stories in this book are true. However, all names have been changed (other than my own name or those of my family members) to protect the privacy of the individuals involved.

❖ ❖ ❖

Chapter One

THE IMPORTANCE OF A DAILY PRACTICE

Unless we maintain a daily practice of connecting with our Spirit, we won't feel its presence and support in our lives. My grace in life was learning early on how to connect with the Holy Spirit within on a daily basis. In fact, I was shown how to make it the foundation of my existence through many practices that have been so reinforced by repetition that they are now woven into the very fabric of who I am.

One of my favorite daily traditions, for example, was first introduced to me when I was a child in Catholic school and reinforced years later while I was a student working with my spiritual mentor Charlie Goodman. The practice was to recite the Lord's Prayer—the Our Father—out loud every morning. I started doing this in the first grade, and it's still part of my regular morning routine. This ritual immediately connects me to my Divine Source, my Creator, and leaves me feeling grounded, balanced, and confident as I begin a new day. Another daily practice is one my mother introduced to me when I was no more than six or seven years old: before I go to sleep each night, I thank my unseen spiritual guides, ancestors, guardian angels, and all Divine helpers for the assistance, support, and blessings they bestowed upon me throughout the day.

These are just two of many practices used for connecting to Spirit that have been handed down to me by my mother; my spiritual teachers and mentors; my wise elders; and at times, by life itself. All have become a cherished part of my being. Some practices I've kept the same, doing them exactly as I was taught to, and others have evolved over the years. The constant, however, is that not a day goes by without my taking the time to anchor my awareness in Spirit, with gratitude and wonder, and ask the great Creator—the Giver of all life—to lead me in this day.

After much reflection on how I've been so lucky to have such an intimate and powerful connection with Spirit, it became obvious that it was the result of my daily focus. Each day (sometimes several times a day), I pray to, invoke, or meditate on Spirit for guidance, direction, and leadership; and then I completely surrender to its force.

Shift in Consciousness

Thankfully, these days more and more people are open to living a spiritually empowered, positive, and peaceful life. We're much more willing to entertain the notion that we create our own reality and aren't simply victims of circumstance, as evidenced by the wildly successful films *The Secret* and *What the Bleep Do We Know!?* We're more willing to explore and even speak with others about spiritual possibilities. And yet, in spite of these encouraging signs, we're still suffering with, and causing some of, the worst personal and worldwide violence and earthly destruction that humankind has ever known.

Incidents of suicide and drug addiction have spiraled out of control, for example. The environment is under siege. Our relationships with each other (and among nations) are blasting apart. So even though the idea of spiritual awakening and personal empowerment sounds appealing and even possible, the actual shift in consciousness we need to make in order to go from victim to Divine co-creator has yet to be made. We all must take a big step forward—if not a leap—to actually jumpstart the transformation that everyone desires and the world so desperately needs.

So how do you remain in constant contact with your joyous, loving Spirit when life doesn't feel joyful at all? There is only one way to succeed in connecting with your Spirit, and that is to make it the most important thing in your life, because it's the endless supply source for all your needs, on all levels. This practice should become as automatic as brushing your teeth or taking a shower. You must anchor Spirit in your life through daily, repetitive techniques such as breath awareness, meditation, setting your intention, expressing gratitude . . . and most of all, surrendering to the flow of life.

Just as plugging a computer into an electrical source gives it the power it needs to run, you must also "plug in" to Divine Source regularly so that your heart remains fully charged. Remember that even though you might be sophisticated and clever, and perhaps are full of ideas and creative expression, you don't generate your own power. No one does. You need to tap into a greater Power Source in order to function at optimal levels. Whether or not you believe or accept it, you depend on a greater source for your life force other than your limited "ego-mind." That power also doesn't come from other people (through seeking their approval), as you probably have been taught in the past.

It's no wonder that people distrust, feel threatened by, and fight with each other. Those who are disconnected from Spirit often tend to manipulate and control others to feed off of their energy in order to sustain themselves. This is achieved through intimidation, guilt, shame, flattery, bullying, and whatever else the ego resorts to. However, authentic power comes from the Divine Creator, who loves everyone unconditionally. When we realize this and begin to plug into this True Source of ceaseless power, we can heal all sense of unworthiness and separation.

With daily practices that reorient your attention away from the fear that arises from the ego, your sense of inner peace returns. When you surrender your attention to this higher force and allow it to direct your life, magic begins. Synchronicity replaces struggle. Doors open instead of close. Your relationships improve instead of break down, and you'll notice that people treat each other like friends instead of enemies. When you connect to Source, you realize there is enough for everyone, so the need to be ready to battle disappears.

This is a huge shift in perception for most people and takes more than just making a decision to fully accept and embody it. Such transformation requires an entire reordering of your life. You must want to make this shift so intensely that you rearrange your priorities, examine and change your beliefs as needed, implement new habits and behaviors, and entertain different thoughts on a daily basis. You must create yourself anew.

The way is not complicated once the decision is made, however. It simply involves a new set of personal priorities and committing to a daily practice of surrendering yourself to the guidance of the Spirit within. Once you do so, your positive personal experiences will provide the motivation to continue. Each day surrendered to Spirit is a day lived as an authentic and holy being, rather than another day endured as an artificially controlled and fearful soul.

If you're ready to reconnect with your kefi—your beautiful, peaceful, holy Spirit—simply decide right now to leave the past behind and commit to the consciousness and daily practice that your transformation requires.

The following chapters will serve as your guide through each of these exciting stages of transformation. They will assist your return to a life filled with Spirit. Remember to take your time and savor each step, for they all bear tremendous gifts. As you progress, you can look forward to the return of your limitless power and light.

Chapter Two

STAGE ONE: AWAKENING TO YOUR SPIRIT

We begin this first stage of transformation relatively unconscious and uninterested in the spiritual nature of the world or ourselves. Our attention is outwardly oriented and focused on the physical world around us more than the world within, and we frequently feel hurried, if not in a full-blown state of emergency over one thing or another. This is mostly caused by the fact that we often unconsciously hold our breath and forget to breathe deeply—creating an inner state of low-grade anxiety, a feeling of "fight-or-flight" in the body.

Before awakening to Spirit, we seek our identity and approval mostly from others and are generally followers rather than leaders. If we do lead, we usually do so by instilling some form of fear in others so that they comply. We tend to manage our lives intellectually, keeping ourselves busy with mostly superficial matters, while underneath we often feel bored, restless, somewhat lost, and frequently ungrounded—as if we aren't really in our bodies. This is why we keep ourselves so busy. It's a way to distract ourselves, at least temporarily, from experiencing the unpleasant inner anxiety that haunts us.

Most of us experience some degree of this spiritually unconscious phase at one time or another, depending on our overall soul development. But it usually comes to an abrupt end with some sort of highly unexpected or hugely upsetting crisis, such as being in an accident, developing an illness, losing a loved one, or feeling rejected by someone we love. It can also result from an anticipated end of a cycle or circumstance—for example, losing a job, graduating from college, leaving a marriage or long-term relationship, starting a new relationship (the loss of single life), or having children (the end of being childless). No matter what actual event or circumstance triggers our awakening, these incidents force us to turn inward and look deeper than we are accustomed to for understanding, reassurance, grounding, and meaning.

Awakening to our Spirit is exciting, but it can also be disturbing—at least from the ego's point of view—so sometimes we might be tempted to continue as if everything were the same. Once the spiritual awakening process begins, however, we cannot ignore it for long. Like a crack in a door opening to an entirely new wing of ourselves and the Universe we inhabit, we are ultimately compelled to see what hidden aspects of life are calling to us.

Once we begin to awaken to our Spirit, we sense possibilities in life that we weren't aware of before and want to find out what they are. As if waking up from an endless dream, we start to look at the world with fresh eyes and a newfound sense of curiosity. We begin to wonder, perhaps for the first time, if there really is more than meets the eye, and if so, we want to know what it is!

Like Humpty Dumpty, once you enter the awakening phase of your spiritual transformation, the world as you know it shatters—never to be reassembled again. And yet you discover that it was merely a shell that hid from you a much greater and more expansive reality that promises rewards, fulfillment, challenges, and peace like you've never known.

So as you're entering the awakening phase and watching your old world fall apart, don't struggle to put it back together. Instead, sift among the pieces for the parts that feel authentic. Look for what might reflect your Spirit, and hold on to only those aspects. Keep in mind that you initialized your spiritual awakening in response to your own internal desire to connect with your true power. In other words, it doesn't just happen to you—although it may certainly feel that way—rather, on a soul level, *you make it happen.*

As you begin the process, know that you're not alone in your transformation. As evolving humans, we are all undergoing some form of higher awakening over and over again. Even those who already appear to be on a spiritual path will continue to discover more of their Divine potential throughout their lives. As long as you are in human form, achieving higher levels of consciousness and personal power is your purpose. Spiritual awakening is a signal that you're ready to learn more about your authentic identity and move into an active state of conscious co-creation with the Universe.

Just as it feels intimidating on the first day of school no matter what grade you're in—from kindergarten to college—you are at this threshold because you've worked your way here . . . and you *are* prepared to cross it, even if it feels uncomfortable at first. You've progressed to the point where the things you've held on to as false security blankets no longer serve you; and you're ready to let go of limited relationships, ideas, and beliefs so that you can be introduced to new, more empowering ones.

As I've said earlier, I've worked with thousands of people over the past 35 years who have shared these types of experiences with me, and I often ask if they were genuinely surprised when their awakening began. Almost everyone I've spoken to said something like: "On the surface, yes . . . but deep down, no, I wasn't surprised. I even felt it coming. I just didn't know when or how."

That description rings true for me, too. I've also had many powerful awakening moments that took my breath away and caught me off guard, but in my heart of hearts, I knew they appeared in direct response to my soul's desire to be more authentic. My soul called these challenges in to support my continuing transformation.

For the most part, what is most shocking for people is how the actual awakening experience commences. It catches us unaware and humbles us in such a way that our intellect (or ego) cannot explain away, minimize, or silence its impact. Awakenings of the Spirit usher in moments of truth and call us back to our true selves. There is no force that can deny the impact of the Spirit awakening.

Once your Spirit taps you on the shoulder, you're compelled to sit up, pay attention, and listen. Like waking up during a restless night, you simply can't go back to sleep.

Keep in mind that this is the first stage of reconnecting with your true power. Some people are very good at putting it off for a while, but eventually, like a computer whose battery is dying, they'll run out of energy by not reconnecting to Source. Allow yourself to open up to something more than your limited ego-based perceptions in order to fuel the kind of profound life experiences you deeply long for and deserve.

The Endless Emergency

I recently spoke with my client Cynthia, who had endured one of the most tumultuous years of her life. She'd lost her job of 23 years; her husband was transferred in his job to another city that was 600 miles away; and she had to go through two surgeries for a slipped disk, neither of which was successful in relieving her tremendous chronic back pain.

In spite of the challenges, Cynthia managed to secure a temporary position in a new company as a training director, which promised to turn into something full-time if she proved herself on the project she was hired to do. Thrilled not to be unemployed, she hobbled to work every day hoping to hide just how debilitated she was, and she fought the good fight against her back pain with large doses of Advil.

Getting into her car on the very morning we spoke, Cynthia realized she hadn't taken a moment to herself in days, maybe weeks, and even our conversation had to be cut short because she was running late for an appointment. Life seemed like an endless state of emergency that she was managing well enough, but the toll of the tremendous stress she was under was exhausting. Cynthia wondered how much longer she could go on before she'd collapse. She was scared.

My client's story is similar to so many other people's experiences that I've been hearing about lately. They're barely managing to get through these rocky times, and it seems to be turning into an epidemic. When I asked Cynthia if she felt safe, she laughed out loud.

"No!" she replied vehemently. "Not now—probably not ever if I think about it." Then she paused and asked very sincerely, "Is it even possible to feel safe in this world?"

"No, not really," I answered. "At least not in the way you're going about it." And that was all because of one simple thing: She wasn't breathing properly. In fact, she was often holding her breath or breathing shallowly throughout most of her day, every day. And because of that, she was disconnected from her Spirit, her fuel for life. That is the only power in the Universe that offers a genuine sense of safety. Without a constant connection to Spirit, my client was doomed, and she intuitively knew it.

Even when Cynthia spoke, she was breathless. While talking to her, I began to feel stressed out and unsafe, too, as I'd unconsciously started to resonate with her "state of emergency" vibration. As sentient beings, we are affected by the vibrations of the people around us, especially the stronger energy of fear and anxiety. If we aren't aware of it, we begin to take on other people's emotional states. We actually stress each other out! Catching myself, I had to momentarily take the phone away from my ear and remember to breathe properly so that I could stay centered, intuitively objective, and free from her anxiety.

"Cynthia," I asked, "do you ever stop and connect with Source energy, with Divine Spirit? You know, to help you move along peacefully during the day?"

"No, not really," she replied. "I want to, but I forget. I mean, I know I should pray, but honestly, I'm so busy that I just get caught up in everything flying at me . . . and before I know it, the day is over and I'm collapsing into bed once again. And to tell you the truth, I don't really know what 'connecting to Source energy' means. How do you do that anyway?"

Now *that* was an honest and relevant question. Like so many others, Cynthia wanted to feel more at peace but had no idea how to make that happen. She'd picked up one or two spiritual books and enjoyed them, but in spite of what she read, very little had changed in her life, except maybe that she now held the hope that change was possible. She wanted me to explain why things always remained the same.

The answer was clear to me, and I shared it with her. I told her that unless we make a conscious decision to connect with Spirit and take action in support of that decision on a daily basis (and the key phrase is *daily basis*), unless we focus our attention and intention on drawing directly from Spirit throughout the day and break our habit of being run by our ego, we remain controlled by those old limited patterns . . . and nothing changes.

Cynthia is like hundreds of people I've met all over the world. I believe we all intuitively know that there is more, but we aren't yet uncomfortable enough to finally get up and open up that door. This is what I call the "early awakening period." It's the rumble before the storm, the shake before the quake that upsets the mind-numbing status quo and gets us moving toward higher awareness.

I had compassion for Cynthia because she, like most of us, lives in a society that promises things on an instant-gratification basis. We order a pizza, and it will be at our doorstep in less than an hour. We go online and can purchase almost anything imaginable and have it delivered to our home with next-day shipping. We turn on the TV and have hundreds of channels to choose from. We're addicted to our BlackBerries, iPhones, and other technical devices that keep us wired to the outer world . . . but how are we supposed to focus on, and tune in to, the inner world?

We don't live in a culture that's supportive of our Spirit. If anything, our world is designed to push Spirit out altogether and numb us with lousy substitutes that keep us addicted and dependent on these "false gods" of the world.

The preamble to our awakening is marked by a growing sense of overwhelm, exhaustion, anxiety, restlessness, impatience, irritation, depression, and complete victimhood. In other words, it's a feeling that life is a struggle, and there's nothing we can do about it.

Making the Shift

Our ego believes that change is death, and it will do everything in its power to avoid it. That's why so many of us remain stuck, telling ourselves that we want a spiritual change yet doing little to nothing about it. We talk a good game but fail to walk a single step on the road to transformation. We promise to read the spiritual books that have been given to us by those who've heard our complaints, or that we've bought on our own accord, but we rarely get through more than a chapter or two before being swept back into the same old drama.

We promise to go deeper and look within but soon forget—that is, until life becomes so frustrating or painful or circumstances change so much that we can no longer stay the same. Talking to others about transformation, even genuinely expressing the desire to experience the peace and personal power of Spirit, is only that: all talk and no action.

Unless and until we take *specific and regular action* and do something to directly connect with our joyful Spirit every day, day after day, until it becomes the central foundation of our lives, nothing will change. Like Cynthia, we will remain enslaved to, and tormented by, the very things that we no longer consciously want. Cynthia's experience proves that, and so does yours.

Being caught up on the "ego wheel" of trying to control life is intoxicating. It feels like you're competing. The game of "keeping things under control" gives you a false sense of power, which is why it can be so enthralling. This becomes all-consuming, especially when your ego actually does manage to keep things in check for a while. You feel a temporary high, an adrenaline rush, which leaves you momentarily satisfied. It's as if you're winning the game . . . but are you, really?

You know the answer. You can't win because the ego's game doesn't end. Ever. It just keeps going and going. No wonder it's exhausting! You can never relax when you're playing the game of control, but you can quit. And when you do, life becomes your own to experience and enjoy.

That is the transformation everyone is talking about these days. To quit the ego game of power, struggle, duality, "me against you," or whatever you want to call it . . . that is the most crucial decision you can make. It can only come about if you do something profoundly different in your life, starting today, and continuing every day until it becomes the only way you want to live.

When we connect with our Spirit, there is no battle to win, no enemy to compete against, and no one who has full rein over us. We must stop struggling with ourselves, each other, and even time. Instead of rushing breathlessly through life, we must breathe the way we did when we were born: fully, slowly, deeply. We must consciously avoid the Spirit-less game of the ego, and remember that those who are playing it are dying—not living.

Asking the Questions

Now take out your journal and turn your attention inward. Contemplate each of the following questions, and invite your Spirit, your most authentic self, to respond to each one. Give yourself plenty of time to feel the genuine response coming from your heart, the source of your power.

- What changes, expected or unexpected, are you facing now?
- Who or what situation are you struggling with?
- In what area do you feel the most stress?
- Do you have enough time in your daily routine to check in with how you feel? What takes up most of your day?

- On a scale of 1 to 10, how much of a "state of emergency" are you generally in?

- What creates a state of emergency in you most often?

- How is your physical health? Do you have any aches and pains?

- How is your energy level? Do you have enough energy during the day, or do you often feel exhausted?

- Do you sleep well? Do you get enough sleep each night?

- Do you make time to do the things you love? Do you actually follow through?

- What thoughts, worries, fears, and/or people are you trying to control?

- Who or what is controlling you?

After writing down your answers, set aside your journal and remain seated. Close your eyes, and calmly breathe in and out through your nose. Start with a sigh or two to help you relax. Feel the energetic tension that racing through life creates in your body. Do you see how it drains your energy, your life force, your kefi, right out of you?

With your next breath, let all of your tension go and simply *be* for a moment or two, even longer if possible. Enjoy sitting and breathing deeply, empty of all thought, free of any agenda, and in the moment. Feel this vibration of being connected to Source. Notice how peaceful, content, and even energized you feel. This is the power of your Spirit, and it's available to you at all times. It is the real you. *Remember this.*

Daily Practice: Notice the Moment

Slow down and take it easy. Unless you're escaping from a fire, there's no need to be in emergency mode. Inhale and exhale through your nose, keeping your mouth closed, and allow this to ease your pace so you feel grounded and relaxed.

Next, set your alarm on your cell phone to go off twice a day. When it beeps (or chirps, vibrates, or whatever type of alarm setting you prefer), stop what you're doing and look around. No matter what is going on, take that moment to notice exactly where you are. Identify the details. What colors, shapes, people, buildings, or animals do you see? Listen to your surroundings. Do you hear others talking, a radio blaring, birds singing, a distant siren? Notice the textures of the things touching your body. What is the surface you are standing or sitting on? Do you feel a warm or cool breeze on your cheeks? Inhale the scents filling the air. Is there coffee brewing, food cooking, or perhaps fresh flowers sitting in a vase? Look in the distance. Is there a smoky haze across the horizon? Continue to gently breathe while experiencing each of your senses. Observation is the gateway to the present moment, a direct link to your Spirit.

The ego mind lives in the past and future, but the Spirit embodies the now. Because the ego isn't in the present moment, it can't initiate new experiences. Engage the power of your Spirit in this moment and choose the kind of experience you want to create today. Decide, rather than hope or wish, by stating it out loud. You are a Divine creator. For example, state that you choose to have an active business day filled with positive phone calls, appointments, and meetings; or perhaps you choose to create an optimistic day filled with gratitude for your friends, family, co-workers, and all the people you interact with. You can do this if you slow down, breathe, and engage in the present moment.

> *"Every breath we take, every step*
> *we make, can be filled with peace, joy,*
> *and serenity. We need only to be awake,*
> *alive in the present moment."*
>
> — THICH NHAT HANH

A Dead End

Robert considered himself a "carefree creative," which really meant that he had no idea who he was or what he wanted to do with his life. At age 22, he had an open heart, a musical soul, and a sleeping Spirit. He didn't think about the future very often, to the consternation of his father, who wanted his son to get a real job (preferably at the sawmill where he worked) and begin a responsible life in earnest.

Instead, Robert spent his time playing conga drums in a band, taking guitar lessons from friends whenever he could, and living off quinoa and laughter. He wasn't serious about much of anything and mostly lived moment to moment—although there were times when, alone at night, he did worry or at least wonder about the future . . . or the fact that he was often broke and had no idea what he wanted to be or do when he grew up, if he ever did.

Nevertheless, each day seemed to somehow take care of itself. And other than being fairly hungry most days, Robert managed to get by and even have fun with his friends. That is, until one day he suddenly experienced such extreme pain in his abdomen that he thought he was going to die and, in fact, welcomed it. The next thing he knew, he was on his way to the hospital, where he was rushed into surgery to remove a burst appendix.

The next two weeks were spent in and out of consciousness, as his body was slow to heal. One morning, he woke up in a full sweat and fever, vomiting so hard he nearly choked to death because he couldn't manage to sit up. The doctor on call immediately sent him back to surgery and reopened the same incision where his appendix had been removed days earlier to discover that a stubborn infection had set in. Robert had to be treated with even more aggressive antibiotics in order to get it under control.

One night, shortly after the trauma of undergoing the second surgery, he slowly came out of his drug-induced daze to see an old Native American grandmother sitting next to him, holding his hand and gently stroking it as he lay there, barely able to move. Disoriented, he looked around the room, not sure where he was or what was happening, and saw several more ancient Native American women sitting near the window surrounded by a beautiful golden and pink halo of light. They all seemed to be watching over him.

Robert looked at the woman gently holding his hand. Although he was barely able to speak, he wanted to understand what was happening. "Grandmother, am I dead?" he asked in a whisper.

"No, Robert," she answered, patting his hand. "God has different plans for you," and said nothing more.

Disappointed because he felt so ready to leave his life, he closed his eyes and tried to connect to the reality of the situation. Still holding the old woman's hand, he suddenly heard another voice: "Robert? Robert? Are you okay?"

It was the night nurse, hovering over him, trying to rouse him. He hadn't rung for her or made any sound to call out for help, yet here she was all of a sudden. Her voice interrupted his connection to the old grandmother, almost as if she were preventing him from slipping out of his body and into death. He felt himself slowly returning to reality: to his hurting body, to the hospital bed, to this world, to his life. The grandmother's touch faded as did the presence of the other grandmothers sitting near the window, and all he could hold on to was her gentle voice in his head. Finally he opened his eyes.

The nurse looked concerned as she studied Robert. He could barely look up at her because he felt so weak, yet he somehow managed to whisper that he was all right. She waited and watched him for another moment; checked his temperature and reviewed his chart; straightened out his bedding; and then slowly left the room, gazing back one more time as if to be sure he was indeed okay.

Now fully awake, all that Robert could do was lie in bed and reflect on what he'd just experienced. Before his encounter with the grandmother, he was in overwhelming pain and had more than once prayed for death to end his suffering. There was nothing significant going on in his life to call him back, and he had no sense of direction or commitment to anything. In other words, he felt like he had nothing to lose by dying. It wasn't really a morose thought, as he definitely wasn't a sullen kind of guy. He just couldn't think of a valid reason to stay. Life felt like a dead end, and he wanted to move on.

However, after hearing the grandmother's words and feeling the gentle caress of her hand on his, a new feeling washed over him. At first, he couldn't quite put his finger on it, but as he sat contemplating what had transpired, it became clear. It was a powerful belief that he suddenly did have a purpose to fulfill, and that God would oversee his life. Never before that moment had he felt such a strong sense of personal worth or that his life mattered . . . so much so that he was being watched over by the gentle, loving force of the grandmothers and that God was actually aware of his existence.

Robert briefly wondered if he'd dreamed the entire thing or if it was a drug-induced hallucination. It didn't matter, though. He knew his experience was real, and it deeply impacted him. That night his world was transformed. He suddenly knew without a doubt that he would recover, and even more important, that his life would change for the better. He didn't know how, but he was absolutely certain that it would. He also felt a powerful fear that he'd always carried (but managed to suppress deep within) swiftly rise up and out of his body. It was gone. He was no longer worried about himself and was more surprised by the intensity of the relief he experienced.

Three days later, Robert was released from the hospital and went home. Until then he had never once thought about Spirit or God, life and death, or purpose and mission. He had never pondered anything beyond the next moment, and this wasn't because he was content or confident about where he was going in life— rather, the unknown terrified and depressed him. Now that the veil between worlds had been pulled back and he was shown the great love and guidance available to him, Robert realized that he wanted to live in a more courageous, conscious way. He looked forward to the future and wanted to make a difference. He remembered what the grandmother had said to him and was committed to fulfilling the "plan" that God had for him.

Robert seemingly stepped back into the world as the same person who had entered the hospital—minus quite a few pounds, which left him looking rather skeletal— but he wasn't the same guy at all. Instead, he returned with a newly discovered, powerful sense of faith in life and in himself, and a clear awareness of a Divine Spirit overseeing all things. He became interested in all things spiritual and opened himself up to every available learning opportunity. He still loved music and played every day, but an entirely new world had revealed itself to him and offered so much more.

It has now been 16 years since that night when Robert woke up in the hospital and was comforted by the grandmother's loving words. Since then, he has established a worldwide healing practice in massage therapy, shamanic journeying, and breath work to assist others in accelerating their spiritual awakening. The foundation of his healing practice is to help pull back the veil between this world and the Spirit world so that other people can also feel the love and guidance that is always available to them.

Until that experience, Robert was headed for a dead end. He truly believes that he "died" in the hospital that night and was mercifully reborn to the far more meaningful and grounded life he loves today. The power of Spirit caught him by surprise, especially because he wasn't particularly looking for it. And yet, noticing how easily he could have continued to drift for years, with no true course of his own, he is humbled and amazed that the Divine Spirit did indeed intercede and set him on the right path.

Making the Shift

Becoming aware of the Spirit realm and all its subtle assistance is an important shift in harnessing the power of Spirit in our own lives. We are not alone in the Universe; and until we become aware of the many faces and levels of Spirit available to help us, we cut ourselves off from the flow of life, which often leads to fear, frustration, and dead ends.

There are so many guardians, healers, helpers, and teachers in the Spirit realm who watch over us and keep us safe. Yet we cannot access their subtle healing support, nor can they influence us or add to our good, if we shut ourselves off to them. We must open our hearts and minds to the reality that the Universe is populated with countless benevolent beings of light who want to assist us. We just need to humble our self-centered perceptions and allow these loving spirits to come through.

We may not see, hear, or touch them, but their influence can always be *felt* through a sudden "Aha!" moment—a breakthrough in insight, an inspired idea, a significant change of direction or heart, or a simple relinquishment of fear.

Asking the Questions

Now take out your journal and turn your attention inward. Contemplate each of the following questions, and invite your Spirit, your most authentic self, to respond to each one. Give yourself plenty of time to feel the genuine response coming from your heart, the source of your power.

- Have you ever suffered an injury, accident, or illness (whether it was physical, mental, or emotional) that seemed to impose a time-out from your ordinary world and wake you up to the more subtle, yet very real and powerful, realm of Spirit? Explain what happened in detail.

- Have you ever experienced a spirit-guided revelation, a sudden shift in perception, or a breakthrough in your worldview or understanding of Spirit? Describe the circumstances.

- Have you ever been inexplicably rerouted or turned around once you realized you were pursuing a dead end? What happened?

- Have you ever experienced direct or indirect contact with Spirit guides, departed ancestors, angels, or other Spirit helpers either during a meditative state, an altered state, or in a dream state?

- Has fear ever suddenly been lifted and replaced with calmness?

- Have you ever felt Divine guidance? Can you remember its message to you? Did you take it to heart?

- Are you still living by the Divine guidance you received, or have you fallen back into a more unconscious state of being that has forgotten the message or has let it fall by the wayside?

- Reflecting on your life today, are you open and receptive, or closed off from and relatively unaware of the more subtle Spirit realm around you?

- If Divine Spirit were to send you a guiding message this very moment, what do you imagine it would be? Write it down.

- Does this message speak to you? Does it resonate in your heart? Can it get past your intellectual resistance and sink in?

After writing down your answers, set aside your journal and remain seated. Close your eyes, and calmly breathe in and out through your nose. Start with a sigh or two to help you relax. Reflect on the vibration in your body after contemplating the more subtle realms of energy surrounding you.

With your next breath, let all of your tension go and simply *be* for a moment or two, even longer if possible. Enjoy sitting and breathing deeply, empty of all thought, free of any agenda, and in the moment. Feel this vibration of being connected to Source. Notice how peaceful, content, and even energized you feel. This is the power of your Spirit, and it's available to you at all times. It is the real you. *Remember this.*

Daily Practice: Connect to the Spirit Realm

Become aware of the energy of Spirit, the powerful yet subtle life force that connects all living things. It is shared throughout the Universe and continues on infinitely. Breathe in slowly and deeply, and relax as you feel the subtle benevolence coming from the Spirit realm to you . . . surrounding, engulfing, and loving you. Think of yourself as warm and protected as a beloved newborn swaddled in a soft blanket. Imagine that this realm is filled with angels, guides, ancestors, nature spirits, teachers, helpers, light beings, joy guides, and other powerful holy forces unknown to you but absolutely available to assist your transformation.

Reflect on the state of your being at this very moment. In what ways would you benefit from the loving support of Spirit guides? What might you ask them through prayer, direct invocation, or a simple request? Make it a daily habit, a regular spiritual practice, to open yourself up and respectfully ask for all available assistance from the subtle realms of Spirit so that you may continue to grow and expand to your highest potential every single day.

> *"He will give his angels charge of you,*
> *To guard you in all your ways.*
> *In their hands they shall bear you up,*
> *Lest you dash your foot against a stone."*

— PSALMS 91:11–12

The Phone Call

Awakening to the power of Spirit can be an intense, dramatic, or even a life-and-death experience such as Robert's, but it doesn't have to be. Your wake-up call can also come in more subtle yet still quite unexpected ways—even in a single moment, as it did for me.

Many years ago when I was in my third year of college, I was living in Denver with my first serious boyfriend. We'd been together for four years and planned to eventually get married. I felt content—that is, until I received a phone call one day from my older brother, Neil, who had just graduated and was about to embark on a career with an airline. Celebrating his new status and ability to travel the world with ease, he said, "Come on, Sonia—let's go to London as soon as you can. I'll use my passes, and we'll have a blast!"

Not only did his words cause me to nearly faint with excitement over such a generous invitation, but they also impacted my Spirit. I felt as if I'd just come alive with all the force of a sleeping giant waking up. I was ready to see the world!

After hanging up the phone, I practically levitated to the other room to share the good news with my boyfriend. "Guess what?" I nearly gasped. "Neil just invited us to go to London with him. Isn't that fabulous?" Fully expecting him to jump for joy with me, I was taken aback when he barely looked up from the TV, and with a genuinely confused look, asked, "Why?"

He might as well have thrown a bucket of ice water in my face, because that was so *not* the reaction I had expected. I was stunned into silence.

I remember thinking, *Why on earth would anyone ever ask <u>why</u> they should go to London?* There was no "why" involved! Who needs a reason to go to London or any other fascinating place for that matter? Adventure, exploration, discovery—that's why . . . at least that explained why for my Spirit.

Looking at each other with equal amounts of confusion, I didn't even try to explain how I felt. I could clearly see that my boyfriend didn't share my feelings. The invitation to explore the unknown didn't speak to his Spirit in the least. I had a realization in that instant, based on his one-word response, that the two of us lived in entirely different universes that would never meet. I simply shook my head at him and said, "Never mind."

Unfazed, he shrugged and said "Okay." Then he went back to watching TV without so much as a glance back at me. Now don't get me wrong. He wasn't trying to be a jerk, nor did he lack a sense of adventure. An avid skier and bike rider, he was also a musician and sang in a band. He was in every way a loving, kind, creative guy; and I really enjoyed being with him. And yet in that moment, I realized that I'd been seriously misguided in thinking that we were two peas in a pod.

I walked back into the bedroom and sat down, still not fully believing what had just happened. More than his not wanting to go to London, I now acknowledged to myself that I was planning to spend the rest of my life with the wrong person. His "Why?" instantly shattered all my illusions that we would have a happy life together. It wasn't because he didn't feel the call to travel or seek adventure. It was because the call was now so strongly awakened in me that the idea of staying in Denver and continuing on the predictable life path we were following—one in which he was content to stay—would kill my Spirit.

I simply couldn't carry on. Like a wild tiger that had been unleashed and needed to run free as fast as it could, my Spirit had been fully awakened by that phone call. I knew I needed to make drastic life changes. I was going to leave the relationship, leave college, leave my family, and even leave Denver so that I could follow my brother into the much bigger, exciting, exotic world that he'd just joined.

This unexpected epiphany made no rational sense at first and caught me completely off guard. Prior to this, I wasn't at all consciously aware that I felt constrained in any way. I didn't talk or dream about traveling, nor did I pine away for far-off places. I had a lot of fun in Colorado doing the same things my boyfriend did, and I wasn't unhappy or restless. It's just that in a single moment, my Spirit woke up to a brand-new vision, and when it did, I knew with every cell of my being that the world I was in and the future world I was planning (including getting married) was not for me and could not happen. Like waking up from a strange dream, I knew with absolute certainty that everything needed to change.

Saying nothing to my boyfriend because there was nothing really to say anyway, the next morning I submitted an application to work for an airline as well. The timing was perfect, and I was interviewed and hired within a week. I had exactly three days to pack my bags and move to Kansas City for training, which meant that I had to quit school, break up with my boyfriend, and move out in that brief time frame if I intended to follow through on all this.

My intellect and emotions were going crazy. *Why am I doing this? How can I be so cruel to break up with my boyfriend and leave just like that? I haven't even finished college! How can I leave Denver? What will I say to my parents? This makes no logical sense.* I continued to chastise myself. I couldn't explain my decision nor could I justify or rationalize it. And I certainly couldn't feel guilt free about it . . . yet I couldn't stop it either. Every cell in my body was marching forward, never for one second hesitating or questioning whether this was absolutely correct for me to do. So I followed my heart and was gone three days later.

Needless to say, the ending at home did not go well. My boyfriend was stunned, hurt, and angry. But one day, after he screamed at me for abandoning him yet again, I quietly asked him, in all sincerity, "Do you really feel this is the wrong thing for me to do?"

My question silenced him, and he didn't speak for what seemed like forever. Then he looked at me with sadness, and said, "No, I don't. Doing what you're doing and leaving is the right thing for you. I'm going nowhere and I know it, but you're going places. This would have happened sooner or later. I'm just sad it was sooner."

I wish I could say that my awakening instantly led to a brilliant life and I lived happily ever after, but it didn't unfold quite that way. Following my Spirit and leaving my home, school, family, and boyfriend in such an impulsive manner rocked my world. Or more accurately, it totally shattered it. I went through all kinds of emotional and even physical confusion, upheaval, and pain in the following months. I had to let my entire identity go and discover a whole new one. After my training in Kansas City, I ended up being based in Chicago, which was utterly intimidating, as was flying all over the country. I was lonely and insecure, but I never, ever once felt that I'd made a mistake. As difficult as awakening to my Spirit was, it was something that I couldn't ignore.

That is how the power of your Spirit works. It pulls, prods, and pushes you to be honest with yourself; remember your soul intentions; face your greatest fears; and reach for your fullest potential. It moves you in the direction of your most authentic self and urges you to commence your soul's plan. No matter where you are in life, if it's not in alignment with your soul's intentions, your Spirit will let you know. It's not always about bringing you comfort and ease; it's furthering your soul's growth, developing your authentic self, and strengthening your connection to your Divine nature. It's about transformation from human to Divine self, which is highly difficult and can be frightening at times. The only thing more frightening, however, is not pursuing your connection to Spirit and remaining disconnected from who you really are.

In my case, my ultimate purpose wasn't working for an airline. In fact, that job served as a stepping-stone to other highly transformational experiences that followed. Yet my awakening made it necessary for me to begin in that way in order to access new opportunities.

The force of Spirit didn't stop with the phone call from my brother that day. It *began* that day. It even pushed me to quit my airline job as quickly as it had persuaded me to apply for it. In the same crazy fashion, it urged me to move to Paris and finish school there, then head back to Chicago. Eventually, my Spirit led me to start on the path of teaching and writing, which at first seemed as irrational and risky as my first move from Denver. Nevertheless, I followed.

Each push taught me more soul lessons and developed within me the skills necessary to fulfill my soul's mission. My Spirit continues to guide me today. It shakes my foundation, rocks my boat, scares my ego, and rewards me beyond my wildest dreams. I've simply learned to recognize it and trust in its power.

Making the Shift

Whether the call from your Spirit comes in subtle prods or radical "come to Jesus" moments of life and death (or both), the key is to know that these calls from Spirit will continue to appear, over and over again, throughout your entire life, always leading you home to Self.

The key is to recognize a call from Spirit and follow it without resistance or hesitation. To do so is to recognize your power and allow it to move you in the direction of your most holy and authentic self. Be prepared for your ego-mind—and other people's egos, too—to resist and even try to attack your efforts to follow your truth. Remember that the ego can't tolerate change, and sometimes even your loved ones react out of the fear that they're losing you.

Remind yourself and those around you that the only thing you do lose is what doesn't reflect or align with your Spirit. Avoid the temptation to ease the discomfort of the process by relying on others for their opinion or approval. To be empowered means to follow your own heart, even if doing so is unpopular or can't be explained to others right now, or ever. Know that you have great support and assistance available to you at all times in the subtle realms, and you're being watched over and loved every step of the way. Still your mind and open your heart . . . and you will feel this holy escort surrounding you right now.

Asking the Questions

Now take out your journal and turn your attention inward. Contemplate each of the following questions, and invite your Spirit, your most authentic self, to respond to each one. Give yourself plenty of time to feel the genuine response coming from your heart, the source of your power.

- What subtle reminders are getting in touch with you, calling you back to your authentic self?

- Where might you be engaged in creating or sustaining something in your life that doesn't feel fully reflective of your Spirit?

- Are you trying to "make the shoe fit" in a relationship, job, or other circumstance, even though you know that your Spirit is not at all in alignment with the situation?

- Where do you feel numb and uninspired in life?

- Have you gotten a "phone call from Spirit" in the form of a conversation that excites you, opens up a possibility that you hadn't considered before, or reveals an avenue that pulls you, even though it might make no logical sense or seem impossible to pursue?

- What would you love to do that your ego (or another person) says is not possible?

- Are you connected to people who stifle your Spirit? Who are they?

After writing down your answers, set aside your journal and remain seated. Close your eyes, and calmly breathe in and out through your nose. Start with a sigh or two to help you relax. Reflect on any energetic burst or shift you may feel as a result of openly acknowledging, without resistance, the call of your Spirit. Feel that distinct vibration coursing through your body and how different it feels from focusing on your intellect alone.

You may discover, as I did, that the course you are on is not in alignment with your Spirit. This may come as a complete surprise or may merely bring to light what you'd been keeping in the recesses of your mind for some time. The awakening process does make you aware of discrepancies and invites you to correct the course. While this can be highly destabilizing to the circumstances at hand, do know that your Spirit seeks to lead you back to your most authentic self. Any other existence would be unfulfilling and uninspiring. Notice what you discover and trust the power of your Spirit to guide you every step of the way, even if it does seem frightening at times.

With your next breath, let all of your tension go and simply *be* for a moment or two, even longer if possible. Enjoy sitting and breathing deeply, empty of all thought, free of any agenda, and in the moment. Feel this vibration of being connected to Source. Notice how peaceful, content, and even energized you feel. This is the power of your Spirit, and it's available to you at all times. It is the real you. *Remember this.*

Daily Practice: Breathe Before You Respond

Learn to take a breath before you speak or act. Take two or three breaths, if possible. Focus your full attention on your heart as you breathe before engaging with the world. One way to remind yourself to do so is to put a rubber band around your wrist and gently snap it from time to time. The physical stimulation will reinforce in your mind that it's important to breathe before you act. Life with breath allows you to respond and create; life without breath causes you to react and feel victimized and powerless.

As you breathe, pay attention to your heart rate. If it seems fast, you might be keeping your body in a fight-or-flight state. If so, continue breathing and give yourself permission to proceed slowly without being rushed. Don't stop until you feel grounded and your body is aligned with your Spirit. Each breath pulls your Spirit more fully into your being and allows it to take over. As easy as it might be to skip practicing this regularly, remember that breath is power. As you feel your Spirit connect with your heart, ask it to take charge and relieve your ego of all duties. Tell your intellect that your Spirit is there to protect you, so you can fully relax. You are safe.

Now let's take it a step further. Empowered by your Spirit and connected to Source, decide with your next breath that you will *not* say yes when you really mean no (and vice versa) when dealing with requests from other people. It's also okay not to answer until you have a chance to breathe deeply and connect with your Spirit to help you discover what the best response is. When that happens, all you have to say is: "I need a few minutes to think about it."

If you feel pressured to respond to someone before you can connect with your breath, then step away for a moment. For example, briefly excuse yourself to go to the restroom or to go outside for some air. Once you're out of the situation, relax and breathe. Connecting with Spirit need not be dramatic—in fact, it's the opposite of drama. It is subtle and calm. It simply requires a moment of peace; a little space; and a few deep, slow breaths. Take these steps and you will succeed.

Do not fear speaking the truth of your Spirit. An authentic response (even if it's a refusal) is surprisingly powerful and respected. What you say may be challenged, but resist the temptation to become defensive. Breathe and be silent instead. By doing so, you'll maintain your connection to Spirit. If necessary, simply repeat your response with love and respect.

Remember that you don't need to look far to connect with the power of your Spirit. It's in all things at all times. Your breath allows it into you! Each day, make a conscious effort to focus on your breathing, for it is the key that unlocks the Divine Source.

"Breathing is the greatest pleasure in life."

— GIOVANNI PAPINI

The Pilgrimage

Patrick was an adventure traveler, an interested observer of the human race, of all things different and unusual. His Spirit was happiest when he was packing his bags and preparing for some far-off destination—the more exotic, the better. He had traveled a lot in his life, especially when he was younger, and he loved every minute of it . . . even the moments when he was extremely uncomfortable. Comfort didn't really matter to him. An adventure was an adventure, and that's when he felt the most alive and vital.

Patrick never used to think twice about dropping everything to get on a bicycle, bus, train, or airplane and heading off into the unknown. He loved it, in fact. Learning something new directly from Source was as good as life could get. He fondly recalled his most amazing experiences, such as the time he was in China and saw people eating monkey brains directly from their crushed skulls. He was simultaneously grossed out and fascinated. *People really did that?*

On the other hand, once when he was in Tokyo, he visited a public steam bath. After a wonderfully relaxing few hours, he stood up to leave only to realize that he was so tall that he could see directly over the wall separating the men's bath from the women's. There he discovered a room full of beautiful naked women lounging around, some combing each other's hair. That was a bath he never forgot! On another occasion, he was riding a horse across an open field in France, when he rode right through the most spectacular cloud of turquoise butterflies that was so thick he couldn't see a foot in front of him.

He never would have truly felt those things by reading a book. He firmly believed that a person had to be there, in the flesh, to have such vivid experiences. That is why he wandered so fearlessly into the unknown. It kept him very much in the present moment.

As he got older, however, Patrick became more "responsible" and less carefree. He got married, bought a house, and had a family. He found himself becoming surprisingly more cautious, even hesitant, when it came to taking off on big adventures. Even though he had his own business and could go whenever he wanted to, he worried that he might lose clients, or that something would go wrong while he was away and he'd regret being gone. He had too much to lose, so he felt as if he couldn't travel as often or as far. It's not that he didn't think about having big adventures. He did. He just didn't let himself be moved enough to act on his desires.

This didn't benefit him or help him stay connected to his Spirit. Getting caught up in his day-to-day life—sitting at his desk for several hours, typing away on his computer, talking on the phone—caused him to become increasingly irritable, negative, critical, and judgmental. This affected the people closest to him, but he was especially hard on himself. He no longer saw the wonder in life.

What he did create, though, was a happy family who loved him very much and could see and feel his Spirit languishing. It wasn't easy to watch or experience this, and it actually frustrated them as well. Finally, as a means to help Patrick recover his Spirit, his wife hatched a plan to send him on the biggest adventure she could conceive of: a trek to Mount Kailash in the Tibetan Himalayas, considered by many ancient religions, including the Hindus and Buddhists, to be the holiest place on Earth and the ultimate spiritual pilgrimage a person can make.

If that didn't resuscitate his dormant Spirit, nothing would. Patrick's family presented this gift to him on Christmas, and he was to leave the following August so he had plenty of time to prepare for his absence from his business as well as get into shape for the rigorous hike ahead. He had no excuse to say no or put it off.

Patrick was speechless and completely surprised. He didn't know what to say. It was just what he needed to revive himself, he thought, and he knew he had his family's support. He gratefully accepted the gift and immediately got excited. Since it was known to be an arduous trek to the 19,000-foot summit (with a high probability of bad weather to boot), he had a big challenge in front of him and was thrilled by it. It felt good to get ready for an adventure. It felt right.

The idea of the trip kept him charged for months, and he told everyone he was going. It wowed them. Tibet sounded so exotic and dangerous, but most of all, it seemed so *spiritual*. Once he started on his journey, however, the reality of his experience was quite different from the fantasies he had carried about it. For one thing, he was traveling with a motley crew, or so he judged at first. They just didn't seem that spiritual, although he had to admit that he didn't appear to be that spiritual either. His primary guide was one of the world's foremost Tibetan scholars, and his partner was a filmmaker. They seemed interesting enough, if a little dry and subdued. The other pilgrims, of whom there were only three, were as different from him as he could imagine. One was an English countess, another a Scottish teacher, and the third a researcher and philosopher from Oregon. *Okay,* he thought, once all the introductions were made, *let the adventure begin!*

They quickly bonded, mostly over the challenging conditions they faced on the mountain, along with the bare minimum of comforts they were given to share once they set out. The mountain path was formidable: jagged, rocky terrain covered in snow, often with water running underneath it. The weather was even worse. The temperatures were well below freezing, while constant stiff winds blew from the north, bringing along with them an unending flurry of freezing snow and rain.

The pilgrimage consisted of walking 52 miles (half of them uphill) to 19,000 feet, at an incredibly slow, grueling pace. To make matters worse, Patrick noted that most of his group clearly didn't read the memo about getting in shape for their trek and had a very hard time trying to keep up. And of course, everyone was affected by the altitude, which made breathing difficult. Patrick felt as if he'd pass out at any given moment. The highlight at the end of each day was getting to camp and resting. They stayed in small yurts and ate yak (and more yak) for all of their meals. (This is a particularly strong, tough meat that most of the country's inhabitants subsist on.) It wasn't something to write home about—that was for certain.

Day after day, Patrick's patience worsened, along with the weather conditions on the mountain. The rest of the crew members were clearly struggling with the altitude, and they were going even slower than the already unbearable pace they had set in the beginning. Patrick thought for sure he was going to become hypothermic if he didn't move faster. Finally, he couldn't take it anymore. He broke free from the group and walked ahead, telling them that he'd meet them at the campsite they were all headed to.

As he started to find his own pace, he began to reflect on what a miserable situation he found himself in. He wasn't having fun, and it certainly wasn't glamorous. It didn't even feel spiritual! It was just hard work in awful conditions with people who challenged his patience. To make matters worse, the fog and clouds were so low that even though he was on the most sacred mountain in the world, he couldn't even see it. He couldn't help but mutter to himself: *Thanks a lot for the gift. What on Earth did I ever do to deserve a punishment like this?!*

As he walked, he became a bit disoriented in the fog and falling snow. He was so cold he worried that he would freeze to death. He longed to be home, in his bed, in the comfort of the wonderful life he had there. Oh, the irony! When he was there, he thought it lacked genuine meaning, but now, with each labored breath he drew in, his home seemed to be the holiest place on Earth. And he missed his family. He came here to receive some kind of spiritual insight, and instead, he was pretty sure that all he would get was a bad case of frostbite.

Is this all there is? he wondered as he inched forward. He wasn't able to let his thoughts float toward spiritual matters. He had to focus on surviving until he got to the next camp, wherever that was. And since he'd been walking for hours, he began to worry about that, too. He should have been there by now.

It was getting later and colder, and he started to think about how he had expected this pilgrimage to somehow make him wiser and more spiritual. He surely wasn't feeling either in the moment. All he could feel was fear, not only because he thought he was going to freeze to death or keel over from altitude sickness (as indicated by the splitting headache he had and the fact the he could barely breathe), but also because a new fear was sneaking in and taking over. He was terrified that he was lost. In fact, he was sure of it.

A new wave of anxiety passed through his nervous system; and he didn't know whether to be angry, pray, turn around, sit down, start running, or laugh out loud. Since the decision was too great to make, he just kept walking straight ahead into the blustering wind.

Eventually his brain froze, or at least he assumed it did because he stopped being afraid. In fact, he stopped thinking altogether and just walked. Almost immediately, things got easier. The outer conditions didn't change; he just stopped fighting against them. It was what it was. He accepted that and settled down and relaxed. *Just keep putting one foot in front of the other,* he told himself. *It has to lead somewhere.* As he continued hiking, breathing the best he could, a miraculous thing happened. He started to feel the Spirit of the mountain, and it was as magnificent as he was told. He couldn't see it, but he felt its power under his feet. It was alive and breathing. He calmed down even more and began to listen to the mountain as he walked.

No longer absorbed in his own mental struggles, he became quite aware and alert. He could feel the Spirit of the blowing north wind. It challenged him to be mindful of where he was going. He could feel the Spirit of the rain and snow washing off his pitiful attempts to control everything. He could even feel the Spirits of the hundreds of thousands of pilgrims who had trekked this same mountain, this very same path before him for thousands of years. His fear lifted, and his mind felt clear and strong.

He continued on for a few short minutes when he saw another pilgrim with his wife and baby in the not-too-far distance. They had stopped and were huddled together. He noticed the pilgrim because he was wearing a brilliant turquoise quilted jacket, and it almost seemed to sparkle against the gray-white backdrop of the mountain. He approached the family and smiled. The man nodded but didn't smile back, and his wife looked at Patrick curiously but didn't reveal anything else. She cuddled her baby, bundled up and bound tightly to her in a sling, and Patrick marveled that she and the child— in fact, all three of them—seemed so calm and serene in such terrible conditions.

Patrick motioned in an attempt to ask if he could sit with them for a while. They nodded and seemed to give off a welcoming energy. They couldn't communicate, as they didn't speak each other's language, so they just sat together in silence. Patrick was glad not to be alone. He could tell by their clothing that they were nomads, people who roamed the lands with their tribe. The man was young, maybe 25 or so, but the lines on his face were already deeply carved, evidence of years of surviving harsh living conditions. But the bright sparkle of his eyes made him seem eternally youthful. His wife looked like a teenager, and although Patrick couldn't see the baby fully, he guessed that the little one was just a few months old.

As they sat together, Patrick remembered that he had a dried yak sandwich in his backpack. Wanting to give them a gift for their kindness, he pulled it out and offered to share it with them. They accepted graciously, and the three of them sat eating their small pieces. After a few minutes, the cold winds kicked in once again, and they all stood up to resume their journeys.

As they walked, the man began to sing a lovely song. His voice was so clear and pure it moved Patrick to his very core. After a few moments, the wife also began to sing, again with a stunningly clear voice that gave a glimpse of her beautiful open heart and sweet Spirit. Not wanting to be left out, Patrick burst into his personal rendition of "I've Been Working on the Railroad" and sang every verse as the pilgrims smiled brightly.

After the impromptu concert, they continued to walk the path in silence, and a thought struck Patrick like a lightning bolt. _This_ _is the gift I'm supposed to receive from my pilgrimage. It's not the mountain, this place, or even the adventure of travel like I thought it would be. It's simply being present, heart-to-heart, with other human beings._

His heart fully expanded, his mind absolutely calm, Patrick was awed by his realization. He took a deep breath and smiled. "What better gift could I ever receive than this?"

Just then, his new friend reached inside his turquoise jacket and pulled out a tiny banana-shaped children's sucker. It had goofy eyes and a silly smile, and looked like it had seen a million miles of trekking in that nomad's possession. The man gazed at it for a moment as if saying good-bye and then handed it to Patrick.

It was so ridiculous that it made Patrick laugh out loud. This is what he came to Mount Kailash for: this silly little smiling sucker! It summed up the entire experience better than words ever could.

Patrick made it to the camp about 45 minutes later, and the pilgrims continued on their way. For the first time since his great journey began, he slept soundly. Three weeks later, he returned to his family and regular life . . . but he wasn't the same man who had left a month earlier. He no longer believed that he needed to do something grand or dramatic in order to live his Spirit. He simply had to embrace whatever was in front of him with his whole heart—instead of fighting it—and connect with a smile, a song if possible, and a sucker.

Making the Shift

Connecting to Spirit isn't necessarily a grand to-do. Rather, it is a subtle, yet powerful, inner experience. You don't have to undergo some earth-shattering spectacle to make a positive transformation, although your ego will certainly try to make you believe that this is necessary. In fact, it will try to convince you that a shift to living a Spirit-empowered life is extraordinarily complicated. Remember that your ego will do anything to stay in control.

The real shift lies in perception. When you stop looking at the world with such a critical view, believing that this is all there is, and recognize and appreciate the wonder of every aspect of life, then the transformation is well under way.

Asking the Questions

Now take out your journal and turn your attention inward. Contemplate each of the following questions, and invite your Spirit, your most authentic self, to respond to each one. Give yourself plenty of time to feel the genuine response coming from your heart, the source of your power.

- What are you most seeking or searching for these days? Do you feel like something is missing?

- Are you resigned to living with this void, or do you feel compelled to fill it?

- Where can you find what you're looking for?

- Are you acknowledging any inner restlessness you feel, or have you tended to avoid it? Where do you think it's coming from?

- How do you spend your free time?

- What responsibilities are you now carrying? Do you feel overwhelmed by them, or are they manageable?

- Do you ever wonder if you're a drag? In other words, do people ever suggest that you take away their fun, leave them feeling drained, or are a real "downer"? Are you? What should you do about it?

- Do you feel connected to spontaneous joy most of the time? Sometimes? Rarely? Never? Explain.

- What do you struggle with most: external conditions or internal ones?

- Do you allow your Spirit to have a voice in your life, or do you forget or ignore it?

After writing down your answers, set aside your journal and remain seated. Close your eyes, and calmly breathe in and out through your nose. Start with a sigh or two to help you relax. Reflect on the vibration you send to others, and the effect their vibration has on you. Notice the distinct energetic differences between the vibration of ego (heavy, tense, contracted) and the vibration of Spirit (light, calm, energizing).

With your next breath, let all of your tension go and simply *be* for a moment or two, even longer if possible. Enjoy sitting and breathing deeply, empty of all thought, free of any agenda, and in the moment. Feel this vibration of being connected to Source. Notice how peaceful, content, and even energized you feel. This is the power of your Spirit, and it's available to you at all times. It is the real you. *Remember this.*

Daily Practice: See the Spirit We Share

Recognize the Holy Spirit in everyone. Look past people's appearances and behaviors, beyond the roles they play in your life, and find the spark of Divine Source dancing in their eyes. Be aware of the stories you tell yourself about others, and resist the urge to judge or label someone. Acknowledge the truth that we all share the same breath of life.

Try this daily practice: First thing in the morning and before retiring at night, stand before a mirror and look yourself directly in the eyes. See the powerful spark of Spirit that resides there. It is the same Spirit you see in others—equally beautiful in all. That is the truth. Once you start doing this regularly, notice how quickly and profoundly your world changes.

"O Holy Spirit . . . descend plentifully into my heart;
enlighten the dark corners of this neglected dwelling,
and scatter there thy cheerful beams."

— SAINT AUGUSTINE

Once we awaken to our Spirit, our perspectives and priorities begin to radically shift. What once felt so important is now less so. What once felt oppressive and confining starts to evaporate and open up. And what we once thought of the world—and most of all, ourselves— begins to shift and expand in more optimistic, promising, and exciting ways. Once we happen upon the sweet calling of our Spirit, connecting to our kefi, we hunger for more. In fact, we often can't think of anything else. We sense the freedom from our anxieties and fears and cannot help but follow the light of Spirit.

Now that we've awakened to the power of our Spirit, we're ready to explore the second stage: *discovery*. Let's move on to the next chapter and continue the journey to our most authentic, empowered self.

Chapter Three

STAGE TWO: DISCOVERING YOUR SPIRIT

The second stage of connecting to Spirit is fueled by curiosity. We usually enter this phase when our ego has exhausted all previous attempts to keep our life under control, and we can't seem to feel happy or satisfied, no matter how good things seem to be on the surface. At this point, we start to look for reasons why this is so. This stage often involves a struggle because we're moving closer to surrendering our ego to Spirit (the third stage), and that can take a long time. In some cases, it never gets resolved.

During this discovery process, most of us tend to connect with Spirit from an intellectual perspective— for example, picking out titles from the spiritual section of bookstores, attending local spiritual seminars, or engaging in discussions about Spirit with like-minded people. And with the enthusiasm of pursuing a new hobby, we often dive into the process with gusto, hopeful that we're on the path to feeling better in our own skin. Our newfound knowledge is empowering, but it also represents an attempt at maintaining control over our transformation. There's a part of us that still doesn't trust the decision to awaken our Spirit and change the way we lead our lives.

The discovery stage, like falling in love, is exciting and intoxicating. It's as if a giant curtain has been pulled back, and we're invited to witness the true workings of life. This is an important stepping-stone to experiencing the power of Spirit because the more we discover our authentic, Divine selves, the more we will naturally want to continue exploring our own potential.

The discovery process can unfold in many ways, some of which may even seem magical. Poignant insights or synchronistic experiences seem to just fall in your lap, allowing you to learn a lot about your Spirit in what feels like the most coincidental events. A book might seem to jump off a shelf in the bookstore, for instance, or you may overhear an enlightening conversation and be drawn in. You could turn on the radio at the precise moment to hear a fascinating interview with an influential spiritual teacher you hadn't heard of before. You may sense that your Spirit awakens for the first time while receiving a massage or during a yoga class. You may even be sitting at the beach, in awe of your beautiful surroundings, when your Spirit activates spontaneously. You might learn about your Spirit as you're caring for your dying mother or when you're training your new puppy. It is as much an organic process as it is an intellectual transition, so be open as you continue on the path to empowering your life with Spirit.

Keep in mind, however, that there's a big difference between learning *about* something and learning via first-hand *experience.* The intellect alone can't help you reconnect with your kefi; it isn't enough to simply be aware of your Spirit. You can only truly learn about your Spirit and what is possible when you make direct contact. Part of the process is to remain open to Spirit through a daily practice. Without doing so, what you choose intellectually will merely stay above your shoulders.

Fear of Commitment

Philip had been a student of mine for several years and was passionate about living a more authentic, spirited life. To that end, we focused on his soul's purpose, his soul's lessons, and the ways in which he could make shifts to better align himself with his creative internal urges.

In the beginning of our work together, he was very excited. He enjoyed the discovery process and was mesmerized by all that he was learning, both about his spiritual nature and the nature of spirituality in general. I gave him a list of books to read to help open his mind and answer the questions he carried in his heart. He loved the material and carried a book with him everywhere he went.

The next step in the discovery of his authentic self, his Divine Spirit, was more involved and took an even greater commitment on his part. I invited Philip to enhance his learning by enrolling in some courses. A few were geared to bringing him closer to his heart's desire, and others were directly related to his interest in landscape design, which he loved but never formally pursued.

Although challenged, he found these suggestions doable. The courses were often only one day in length or during a weekend, so he could easily fit them into his schedule. The nearby community college offered classes in landscape design one night a week, so he didn't have any trouble making time for that either.

When we touched base again, Philip expressed a desire to move even deeper into his authentic, empowered Spirit. This time I assigned him a daily practice consisting of breath work, yoga, stretching, and meditation. He was eager to get started, and when we parted, he'd committed to not only go inward but to also anchor his day-to-day life in connecting with his Spirit.

We spoke again a few months later, and the minute I heard his voice I could tell he was unsettled and frustrated. His job as a consultant was going well enough, but he wasn't 100 percent confident that he could trust the people he worked for. At the same time, a former client wanted to hire him as an employee, and a good friend was proposing that they form a partnership together. With all of these options dancing before his eyes, he'd lost his bearings and needed my guidance.

Before I suggested anything, I asked Philip if he was making the effort to connect with his Spirit every day through the daily practices I'd assigned him.

He paused and then said, "Well, I fully intended to. It's just that this is my busiest time of the year, and I can't commit to anything right now."

I didn't respond right away so that he could hear his own words resonate in the world. "So," I replied, "just to make sure I understand . . . you called me because you can't seem to get clear guidance from your Spirit, and you can't connect with your Spirit for 30 minutes a day because it's not convenient. Although you want to experience the guidance and power of your Spirit, you don't have time to connect with it because other things are more important at the moment. Is that right?"

Philip burst out laughing. "Yes, I guess that's exactly what I said! I can't believe I said it, but it's true." He was genuinely surprised to see his reluctance to connecting with his Spirit so clearly mirrored back to him.

"I had no idea until this moment just how resistant to being in silent connection with my Spirit I am. Wow! What a shock! Why is that?"

It was a good question, and one we must all ask ourselves. Reading about our spiritual selves is quite different from actually connecting on a daily basis. Philip's resistance, perhaps every person's resistance, lies in the need to shift priorities in order to move forward. This invites the possibility of discovering that what we're doing isn't in alignment with what our Spirit wants. Admitting that we may need to make significant changes in life can be difficult.

So the mind (or ego) rationalizes reasons to avoid the Spirit, because what our Spirit reveals is often inconvenient. In Philip's case, he avoided connecting with his Spirit on a daily basis because his ego convinced him that it would be a waste of time and he was too busy anyway. But underneath those superficial rationalizations, he and I quickly uncovered something deeper. By regularly tuning in to his Spirit, he might have to face the deeper truth that he didn't want his job and would much rather become a full-time landscape gardener. This scared him, though.

That reality wasn't financially sound. How could he make a living and pay his rent? A cascading litany of concerns clouded his thinking. He feared that being authentic was too expensive, impractical, and unreliable, so he avoided the invitation to go inward. He blamed his busy life, but in fact, he made his life busy so he wouldn't have to think about his soul's calling. The idea that connecting to Spirit would be complex and financially risky made it easier for him to turn his back on his authentic self.

I'm writing about Philip's fear because in my private practice as an intuitive guide, this is the number one problem I encounter with clients. While we want to transform into spiritual beings, we fear the effort may be too complicated and the rewards not guaranteed. So we learn enough to talk about it, but stop short of experiencing it in the most direct way—through a committed daily practice, because this is where "the rubber hits the road." We have to make real changes that may feel risky. The paradox is that connecting with Spirit regularly teaches us that the risks are only risks to the ego, and the more we connect with Spirit, the more empowered we become. We can only discover this, though, by learning it directly through our own experiences.

Many people do fear deep down that connecting with Spirit and following their truth will completely deconstruct their lives. That rationale isn't entirely off base. If you've built your life on fearful choices that have led you away from your authentic self, you know it. And you also know deep down in your heart of hearts that the minimum amount of genuine focus inward will most definitely make you painfully aware of this.

Yet what you don't realize is that the Spirit within isn't a "gotcha" machine, ready to pounce and point out your mistakes. Rather, your Spirit is the unlimited, unconditionally loving, creative inner spark that nudges you toward your highest good with brilliant suggestions, bright ideas and guidance, and generous solutions . . . all aimed at redirecting your life to flow with your Spirit.

Running away from or resisting this profound personal connection with the Source within your Spirit is just the ego's way of not surrendering to or trusting the larger empowered aspects of yourself. The trouble, though, is that if you refuse to connect with your Spirit in a consistent way, your life patterns and problems won't shift or improve. It is only by surrendering to Spirit in a daily practice of breath work, meditation, and perhaps a few yoga stretches that you will be able to connect with the power and guidance of Spirit. Your Spirit doesn't bring misery—it disrupts misery and ushers in truth.

Philip and I explored his resistance further to get to the truth. We uncovered his hidden desire to go in the direction of landscape design full-time, which was something his Spirit wanted, although he was sure it wouldn't support him the same way his consulting job did, if at all. By inviting Philip to breathe past that resistance and go deep within to seek guidance from his Spirit, a new door opened for him.

After just a few meditative deep breaths and turning inward to his heart and Spirit, he had a new insight. He could start a career in landscaping while keeping two or three strong clients until his new business became stable. The minute he admitted what his Spirit genuinely wanted, the way was shown. But until he made the connection, all he got was confusion, stagnation, and frustration—none of which did anything but exhaust him.

Making the Shift

Connecting with your Spirit through breath work and meditation is absolutely critical to empowering yourself. You can't get around this truth: until you invest in your Spirit, it cannot invest in you.

The ego-mind wants you to believe that time spent focusing on your authentic self isn't important, and it will do everything to keep you distracted. After all, doing so would potentially change everything. (And you know that the ego hates change!) Your Spirit will challenge everything that isn't genuine or in alignment with your Divine self. Once you're fully awakened, you'll have the confidence to trust your Spirit to guide you so that your life can flow in peace.

The power of your Spirit is first felt when you decide that a daily practice grounded in connecting to your Divine self is the only way to live. This is affirmed by the words of the brilliant spiritual teacher Andrew Cohen (from his book *Embracing Heaven & Earth*):

> Of course we don't know how many of us are actually going to succeed in becoming enlightened in this life. We can never predict these things. But the question of how many of us are going to come to that point in our own evolution where we are willing to do *anything that we possibly can* in order to succeed is a very different matter. You see, the power to go that far lies in our very own hands. And in the end, there is nothing more that any of us can do than want to be

free more than anything else and be willing to back it up with action and with sacrifice. From a certain point of view, whether or not we actually succeed in becoming fully enlightened doesn't really matter. It doesn't make any difference. But what does make all the difference in the world is whether or not we are *truly willing now.*

Asking the Questions

Now take out your journal and turn your attention inward. Contemplate each of the following questions, and invite your Spirit, your most authentic self, to respond to each one. Give yourself plenty of time to feel the genuine response coming from your heart, the source of your power.

- Do you have a regular spiritual practice?

- Do you actually make time to perform this practice or ritual every day?

- Is it something that you feel you must do, or do you truly love doing it? Perhaps both?

- In what ways do you connect with your Spirit?

- Do you begin your day by connecting with your Spirit?

- Do you focus on your Spirit during the day?

- Do you end your day by connecting with your Spirit?

- Are you willing to connect with your Spirit through daily meditation, breath work, and yoga?

After writing down your answers, set aside your journal and remain seated. Close your eyes, and calmly breathe in and out through your nose. Start with a sigh or two to help you relax. Take note of the vibration in your body after contemplating how your life might change if you begin a daily practice of centering yourself through your heart and Spirit. Feel the unlimited freedom in looking to Source for support—and not relying upon others.

With your next breath, let all of your tension go and simply *be* for a moment or two, even longer if possible. Enjoy sitting and breathing deeply, empty of all thought, free of any agenda, and in the moment. Feel this vibration of being connected to Source. Notice how peaceful, content, and even energized you feel. This is the power of your Spirit, and it's available to you at all times. It is the real you. *Remember this.*

Daily Practice: Try Connected Breathing

As simplistic as it sounds, *breathing* is the only action that can interrupt and actually end the ego's game of fear and control. You can reset your personal vibration to a more creative, empowered, and joyful level. Not only did Philip need to stop denying or suppressing his true desires, but he also needed to breathe in a way that would help quiet down his ego. Then his attention could immediately shift to a higher, more peaceful frequency. Breath is how the transformation from fearful ego to expanded, joyful Spirit begins. It's necessary to regularly practice and engage in conscious, mindful breathing until it becomes a habit.

My favorite breathing technique to connect with my Spirit is called *connected breathing,* and I do it every morning. Here's the process: Wake up 15 minutes earlier than you normally would. Sit up in bed, with your back against a pillow. If possible, set your alarm to ring after 15 minutes, so you can relax and focus without worrying about running late.

Close your eyes, and take a few deep breaths in and out through your nose to gently wake up your body. Pull your breath even more deeply into your abdomen by relaxing your diaphragm as you inhale. Then quickly release your breath by relaxing your muscles, as if letting out a sigh. (Continue breathing through your nose, keeping your mouth shut.) Don't force your breaths either way, but do be aware of allowing each inhalation to enter deep into your belly, and then releasing it easily and quickly.

As you breathe, connect the end of each inhale with the beginning of each exhale, and vice versa, so that there is no pause between breaths. It may feel odd at first, especially since you're probably used to unconsciously holding your breath. By connecting your breathing, you also connect to the nonstop flow of Divine Spirit, and this is what changes your vibration. Soon you'll get used to this technique and will enjoy the way it makes you feel.

It helps to visualize your breath flowing in and out of your body as a swinging pendulum: inhale, breath swinging in; exhale, breath swinging out. Imagine your breath flowing easily and peacefully in and out of your lungs, over and over again, without interruption, for 15 minutes.

With practice, you'll enter a trancelike state. See yourself pulling in Divine love with every inhalation, energizing every cell with vitality and holiness. Feel how receptive and relaxed your body is. As you exhale, do so gently and without force. Imagine releasing all the toxins circulating in your system back into the atmosphere, along with any anxiety, stress, worry, toxic thinking, negative past experiences, and free-floating fears of the future that reside inside you. See each exhale energetically purging all vibrations that no longer serve a useful and joyful purpose in your life, and each inhale fueling your authentic self in every way.

Know that your flowing breath is cleansing you, inside and out, creating a cocoon of brilliant life-giving energy all around you. Feel the shift in vibration that it creates. The deeper and longer you focus on your breathing, the clearer your body, mind, and emotions become. This leaves you relaxed, peaceful, and fully grounded in the present.

Continue this breath work until the alarm rings or you naturally feel ready to enter the day. Then place your hands gently over your closed eyes, and focus on the peacefulness flowing through your body. Don't rush or change your breathing pattern. Slowly open your eyes. Then with a final deep breath, pull your hands away from your eyes. Stretch, stand up, and resume normal breathing.

As you start the day, feel how you're fully supported by the Divine love and joyful spirit of Source, your Creator. You don't need to seek nourishment and support from people and circumstances around you, so there is no need to fear or feel insecure. They are not your Source; they share Source energy but do not provide it for you. Breath is your Source! Focus on your breathing whenever you are uncomfortable or in doubt of yourself; and you'll return to this peaceful, holy state of being.

> *"A mortal lives not through that breath that flows in and that flows out. The source of his life is another and this causes the breath to flow."*
>
> — THE UPANISHADS

A Gut Feeling

Andrea was raised with her twin sister and two other siblings by highly intellectual and politically active parents who lived and worked under the umbrella of the University of Chicago, a world-renowned academic institution. She loved reading, learning, and engaging in lively debates with a diverse group of teachers and students from around the world who often stayed in her family's home for weeks or even months at a time.

As a child, Andrea was independent, outspoken, and creative. From the age of 6 through her early 20s, she studied professional dance. It was her passion. She was excited to embark on a life of dance after college, until her mother commented that it was time for her to get a "real job" after graduation. Dejected, Andrea simply hung up her dancing shoes and shut the door on something she truly loved. Thus began what she called her "lost years." She drifted from one job to the next in several nonprofit agencies, trying to engage in "meaningful" work. But each experience was more devoid of life and genuine meaning than the last.

Refusing to indulge her dissatisfaction any longer, Andrea forged ahead in search of a career she could really connect with. Drawing upon her activist interests, she finally decided, after 20 years of frustration and periods of unemployment, to return to school and pursue a degree in public policy. This ambition satisfied her ego's need to attain something of "social substance" and gave her a sense of purpose. Acting on this decision, she immediately went back to her roots and applied to the graduate school at the University of Chicago. To her utter shock, she was accepted into the program.

Once the glamour and excitement of this impressive accomplishment wore off, the real work in beginning a new path commenced. To Andrea's horror, what she actually encountered wasn't the meaningful, nurturing work to help shape the world that she had expected; rather, she faced a mountain of sterile, dry intellectual and mathematical studies, which didn't at all connect to her interests.

To exacerbate the situation, she began to experience flare-ups of intense digestive trouble, something she'd dealt with in the past but had managed to get control of. Almost overnight—shortly after her commitment to the public-policy program—her physical health completely broke down. She couldn't eat a single morsel of food without experiencing severe abdominal pain. She had allergic reactions to foods, chemicals, and sometimes even the air itself. In addition, she couldn't sleep, she had no energy, she noticed that her hair was falling out, and she had asthma attacks. She was basically incapacitated.

Andrea became so ill she had to temporarily leave the graduate program and fight for her life. At one point, she turned to her twin sister and said, "I'm dying. Every part of me—mind, body, and soul—has collapsed. I can't get myself to rally or turn it around like I've done before."

For the next two years, Andrea's sole focus was on getting well. She visited ten separate doctors, all specialists, in the hope of receiving a diagnosis and cure. Instead, she was given ten different opinions, ranging from having multiple sclerosis to suffering from depression to making the entire thing up.

During this time, Andrea had held on to her public-policy ambitions, but she repeatedly confided in her sister that it appealed more to her intellect than to her gut feeling about what she should dedicate herself to. Not making the connection between life direction and her illness, she toiled on looking for answers. Finally, she met a holistic doctor who correctly diagnosed her illness as a case of "leaky gut," put her on a massively restricted diet, gave her a ton of books to read, and suggested she begin acupuncture in place of medication to control her symptoms since the medications weren't working.

That meeting changed her life. With the correct diagnosis, she finally relaxed, intuitively sensing that help was on the way. Still unable to return to school, she stayed home and read everything her doctor gave her about her condition. Then she read books on nutrition; holistic healing; and getting in touch with her Spirit, her ultimate Source of vitality. In the process, an entirely new world slowly unveiled itself to her. The things she was learning, along with a gradual improvement in her health, began to make a difference in her, both inside and out. She was starting to heal not only her body, but also her restless, anxious, "got to do something meaningful right now," intellectually driven mind as well.

As she became stronger, Andrea began to review her life from a new perspective, one that approached her physical health as a reflection of her spiritual health. She could trace the early symptoms of her poor health all the way back to the very week she walked away from dance, her first love, and shut that door to her Spirit. The more she pursued interests and jobs that only appealed to her intellect (and completely ignored her authentic self), the more frequent and worse her symptoms became.

One day, soon after a particularly healing session with her acupuncturist, Andrea called her twin sister and said she needed to come over. Once there, not even sure what she was thinking, let alone what she was going to say, she suddenly blurted out, "I don't want to return to the University of Chicago and study public policy. I think I want to study acupuncture and research this path instead."

Her own words surprised her. She didn't know she felt that way! After all, it was completely different from anything she'd ever done or expressed interest in before. Yet, now deeply immersed in her healing journey, she realized that these words were the first she uttered that felt right in her gut. In fact, once she announced her feelings out loud, her entire body buzzed with a burst of energy, as if to say, *Yes! That's so true!*

Andrea's sister didn't miss a beat. "Look at you. You're beaming! There's a light in your eyes that I haven't seen for at least two years, maybe more. I think it means that quitting the university path and studying the alternative is exactly what you must do. Follow that inclination!"

And that was that. Andrea's decision was made. But more than that, for the first time in her life, it was a decision made by her Spirit—her authentic self, and not just her intellect wanting to impress her family. The following day, she withdrew from school and signed up for training in acupuncture and Chinese medicine. At 50 years old, she'd never felt more alive, passionate, and enthusiastic about her life as in that moment.

A year later, Andrea's body had completely recovered, and the light in her eyes had grown brighter than ever. She loves her training program, which is demanding and rigorous, but truly aligned with her Spirit. She's even thinking about starting her own practice. When talking to her over dinner recently, I asked her exactly what had happened to cause her to completely change her path.

She paused for a moment and then said, "From the time I was young, my world was centered on the intellect. Feelings weren't highly regarded, and 'Spirit' was something I didn't accept or believe in at all. I guess I confused it with religion, and wouldn't ever entertain such superstition as an intellectual person. And yet, it took me nearly dying to open my mind and heart to what I'd denied for so long.

"Don't get me wrong. I still love science, activism, and health care; and I'll always have an intellectual mind-set. I just discovered that there was a missing component: listening to and following my heart. When I discovered that, my life began healing from the inside out. I hadn't allowed Spirit in my life, and in doing so, I began to die. But once I opened up to my feelings and began to learn about my Divine self, everything started to improve."

We all eventually reach a moment in life when we must come face-to-face with a force greater than our ego, or intellect; and at that point, we're invited to recognize the holy force, the Spirit. People struggle against this because it feels as if we're being asked to hand over our power. On the contrary, it's actually an invitation to get to know and accept the most powerful, brilliant, authentic essence of ourselves.

For some, this moment of recognition comes with little drama; for others, it arrives with a bang. I personally view the ego the way it's depicted in the classic tarot card "The Fool." This character represents your Divine Spirit as it's about to step off a cliff and embark on the human journey. At the Fool's feet is a small white dog, which represents your intellect. The trouble is that, for most, the intellect is far more demanding than an agreeable little pup. In Andrea's case, her intellect morphed into the equivalent of an untrained beast, always poised to attack her Spirit and banish it from her life.

To embrace the power of your Spirit, it's up to you to contain, restrain, and then train your intellectual self to support rather than attack your Spirit. Remember that Spirit is not an invader, an interloper, or a lesser god to be dismissed and ridiculed. Spirit is the holy essence with all the Divine breath of life that makes consciousness possible. Understanding that is the most intelligent and enlightened discovery you can make in life. To humble yourself to Spirit is to humble your mind to its true master—your Divine nature. In doing so, both mind and Spirit enter into the sacred marriage of mind and heart, and profound personal peace begins.

Making the Shift

As you know, to connect with your Spirit, you must awaken to it and then go through a discovery phase so that you know and trust what you're connecting to. However, don't turn this into a battle of conquering your ego. Remember that your ego simply needs to be reeducated in order to better serve its true master—your Divine self.

During this discovery stage, it's important to become an open and willing student as you're guided through many learning channels. This is the time to follow all impulses to read books on the subject of Spirit, attend lectures and seminars, go to weekend workshops, listen to live webcasts hosted by spiritual teachers and thinkers, and enroll in ongoing classes that call to you. Keep yourself open to new information coming your way through all avenues.

You may feel as if it's a coincidence that certain events or learning opportunities are suddenly becoming available to you, but the truth is that they were there all along. You simply hadn't yet embraced the discovery phase of your spiritual transformation. Yet, as it's been said, once the student is ready, the teacher (in all its forms) appears. You are now stepping through the doorway of Spirit, preparing to enter the flow.

Follow all impulses and be open to everything. Don't look for what is "right." In the realm of Spirit, there is no right or wrong. The question to ask yourself is: *What feels true for me right now?* Look inward and wait for the answer to come from your heart. Step out of your comfort zone, and embrace being a student of Spirit.

Asking the Questions

Now take out your journal and turn your attention inward. Contemplate each of the following questions, and invite your Spirit, your most authentic self, to respond to each one. Give yourself plenty of time to feel the genuine response coming from your heart, the source of your power.

- What understanding or perception of Spirit do you hold today?

- What part of this perception originated when you were a child? Has it evolved over time?

- Do you view the power of your Spirit as a flowing part of who you are, or do you see it as something outside of yourself? Do you want to feel your Spirit but don't know how?

- In what way is your Spirit trying to get your attention today?

- What might your Spirit be conveying to you that you are ignoring or aren't giving your full attention to?

- Do you feel a conflict between your Spirit (your most authentic self) and your intellect (your ego)? If so, can you describe this discord?

- Do you carry strong ideas about the way you "should" or are "supposed to" act or behave? Are these feelings subtle or intense?

- Have these internal conflicts been around for so long that they feel "normal," or are they something you've been feeling more recently?

- Do you feel the urge to expand, create, or express yourself more? Do you spend lots of time trying to figure things out mentally to no peaceful avail?

- Do you take time to turn within and be quiet? Do you tune in to your Spirit and feel its influence?

After writing down your answers, set aside your journal and remain seated. Close your eyes, and calmly breathe in and out through your nose. Start with a sigh or two to help you relax. Reflect on the vibration in your body after contemplating the conflict between ego and Spirit.

With your next breath, let all of your tension go and simply *be* for a moment or two, even longer if possible. Enjoy sitting and breathing deeply, empty of all thought, free of any agenda, and in the moment. Feel this vibration of being connected to Source. Notice how peaceful, content, and even energized you feel. This is the power of your Spirit, and it's available to you at all times. It is the real you. *Remember this.*

Daily Practice: Peel the Onion

Uncovering the power of your Spirit is like peeling away the layers of an onion. Each layer represents what is not your authentic self. Practice connected breathing, and visualize what might make up your layers. Your outer layer might be anger or anxiety, for example. Peel it away with your breath. Maybe the next layer is control or frustration. Again, breathe deeply and peel that away as well. The next layer might be confusion or fear. Continue peeling away each layer of energy that's occupying your mind—one at a time—until you reach your heart, your Spirit.

The layers may peel off quickly, or they might barely budge. Don't worry about it—just notice where the layers stop; and whether it's a thought, feeling, belief, or old pattern controlling you at the moment. When you hit a block, sit with it, breathe into it, and observe it as if you were a witness. Pay attention to the energy and how it controls you. Notice how your pattern of thought feels, too. Your ego keeps you stuck in patterns that cause energetic contractions, inhibiting your breathing and interrupting the flow of life. Watch these patterns as you continue your breath work.

If you're experiencing particularly intense emotions (such as anger, fear, insecurity, sadness, or anxiety), simply keep breathing and see how breath and awareness affect them. Do not act on the energies engulfing you; remember to just observe. Notice that with each inhale and exhale, you're putting more space and light between yourself and these intense thoughts and feelings.

Do this for a minimum of three to five minutes (ten if possible). This is usually enough time to break free of the trance of the ego patterns. The quiet observer is your Spirit. With each breath of awareness, you'll realize how much stronger, brighter, and more powerful your Spirit becomes. Each breath ushers in more space and light, releasing you from the grip of negativity.

By practicing observant awareness every day for a few minutes, you'll develop an automatic response to detach and expand into Spirit rather than contract and engage negative energies as they arise. Be patient in the beginning. Shifting from ego to Spirit takes time. Your responses won't change overnight, but with consistent practice you'll see a difference in about 40 days. (A 40-day duration is mentioned many times throughout the Bible and represents a full season or cycle of change. In practicing for a full 40 days, you override your old patterns and establish a new imprint from an unconscious, ego-centered, disempowered mode of living to a Spirit-centered, conscious-choice-directed mode of living.)

When the shift to Spirit does begin, you'll experience a remarkable liberation from being unconsciously controlled by unwanted ego patterns. The more you apply observant breath to your thoughts, the more quickly you will break free from unproductive negative thoughts and enter the clear, expanded, creative space of your Spirit.

"Oh, would that my mind could let fall its dead ideas, as the tree does its withered leaves!"

— ANDRÉ GIDE

Better Than Disneyland

Lexy's life was simple, and she never questioned the way things were. Born and raised in a small rural town in Tennessee—in the heart of the Bible Belt—she followed the strict rules of her Baptist upbringing. She worked in an office after graduating from high school and never went to college. At 19, she married John, a nice guy she'd met in church, and had three beautiful children with him, one right after the other.

Her life as a stay-at-home mom was her world, and as far as she knew, this was what life was all about. So Lexy was happy . . . until one day, just moments after her husband called to say he was on his way home from work, a large tractor unexpectedly pulled out in front of his car, causing a terrible accident. John died instantly, and so did everything that Lexy knew or believed about life.

She felt stunned, confused, abandoned, and devastated. This wasn't what her life was supposed to be like. According to the "life script" she was taught and followed obediently, she and her husband were supposed to raise their kids together and take vacations at the lake each summer. John was going to coach Little League, and she would host the kids' birthday parties. They would add on to the house and grow old together. But now all that had disappeared. Without her husband, Lexy felt as if she could hardly function. Her world had been torn apart, and life would never be the same again.

Fortunately, her husband was well insured, so at least Lexy was able to meet the family's financial needs without further destabilizing all of their lives. She just had to pick up the shattered pieces of herself and put them back together again—and fast, because her kids needed her. She just didn't know where or how to start doing that.

The town where she lived offered little support or comfort. It seemed in many ways that her neighbors were far more interested in gossiping about the accident—whispers of "the poor thing" seemed to follow her everywhere—than they were in actually helping her regain her footing once the funeral was over.

It's not that they weren't nice people. They just didn't know how to comfort her after such a shocking tragedy, so they avoided her instead.

Lexy found even less support at her church. Every time she went, it seemed as if all she heard about was sin and damnation, but next to nothing about heaven. Where was her husband now that his life was over? Was he in hell, as her preacher suggested? How could that be? Her anxious thoughts consumed her and became so disturbing that they even gave her nightmares. She stopped going to church, even though that gave the town's residents something else to gossip about.

Never once before this accident did she even think to question what she'd heard from the pulpit every Sunday throughout her entire life. But after John died, she couldn't listen to a word of it. Something inside her told her that it just wasn't true.

So Lexy was on her own to figure out what was true so that she could escape this nightmare, but she didn't know where to start. She began her search for understanding and a way to connect with others in the most accessible place she knew: *The Oprah Winfrey Show*. One day while watching, the show featured a few guests who had appeared in the movie *The Secret*. Lexy listened to them discussing "the Spirit within," which was a radically new concept to her. The only Spirit she knew of was the Holy Spirit, whom she greatly feared and would certainly never be so audacious as to consider it a part of herself, as these people were suggesting. She wasn't worthy—no one was. It was almost heretical.

Intrigued, and fueled by her pain and a need for answers, she overcame her hesitation to explore what they were talking about and ordered the movie as well as some of the books that were also discussed on the show. On that day, the door to the nonphysical world cracked open for Lexy. The heaven and hell she was taught to believe in slowly began to disappear, and she took the first steps toward courageously pushing past her fears and hesitations in search of her husband's Spirit so she could at least say good-bye and find some closure.

The discovery process commenced. One spiritual book led to another and another, until Lexy had read all that the local bookstore had to offer (which wasn't much). She moved her search on to the Internet, looking for more material from which she could find answers. Not only did she become a voracious reader of all things spiritual—including life after death, reincarnation, how thoughts and beliefs shape our lives, positive manifestation, and more—but she also began to subscribe and listen to countless online radio shows featuring all kinds of exciting and enlightening interviews relating to spirituality.

The more she learned, the more she wanted to know. Each tidbit she picked up about the world beyond the physical and the notion of a Spirit within eased the gaping wound in her heart a little more. Although she was finally beginning to feel better, she soon discovered that her newfound views couldn't be shared with others. In fact, people in her town thought she'd lost her mind and her religion; and she was either crazy, possessed by the devil due to the emotional trauma from the accident, or just plain weird. Her neighbors smiled politely when face-to-face with her, but many gossiped even more the minute she was out of earshot.

Lexy's pain, however, was too great for her to worry about what others thought or try to regain their approval. She was sinking, and her kids needed her to stay afloat. Following her intuition and learning all she could about spirituality was the only thing that helped, and it helped her a lot.

Although her mind had calmed somewhat knowing that everyone has an eternal, holy Spirit that doesn't die, she didn't feel the Spirit *in her*, but she desperately wanted to. In fact, she needed to, so she decided to search for ways to succeed in her quest no matter what it took. She had to feel the Spirit within so she could teach her kids to feel it, too. Then they'd never be as afraid of, and as unprepared for, sudden change and death, as she had been. She never wanted them to go through the hell she was slowly starting to come out of. She realized that she could never prevent her children from facing sorrow and loss in life, but she could at least equip them with the spiritual wherewithal to know how to deal with it so it wouldn't destroy them as it almost did her.

Lexy pushed herself even further into the unknown and stepped out of her comfort zone by enrolling in several online spiritual classes so that she could connect with others with similar interests. She chatted with people from all over the world, many of whom were also enduring dramatic life changes, which confirmed that she wasn't alone or crazy—something she had wondered about from time to time.

Soon, however, even web classes weren't enough to satisfy Lexy's relentless curiosity and insatiable desire to know her Spirit. She started feeling claustrophobic in her small town and wanted to be with others she could share and compare ideas with in person. So doing the unthinkable for mothers in her community, she left her kids with her mother and went to a weeklong seminar on spirituality and intuition in upstate New York, all the while mindful of the gossip and scorn that trailed in her wake.

Miraculously, she didn't care. Her heart was healing; her world was expanding; and even more exciting and unexpected, she actually felt closer to her husband in Spirit than she ever had when he was alive. They'd never had an intimate conversation while he was alive, let alone one about Spirit. It simply didn't come up because they weren't aware of it. Now, every night, she could connect with his Spirit in her heart and feel his presence, however subtle and fleeting. She no longer doubted. He was helping her from the Spirit realm to awaken her own Spirit before she died.

Maybe that's why he died so suddenly, she thought one day. *He really is helping me, and with all that I'm learning, perhaps I can open the boys up to a richer, more wonderful world than he ever had.*

Propelled by a force seemingly greater than herself, she went from classes and seminars to working personally with gifted massage therapists, energy workers, clairvoyants, intuitives (where she met me), and even shamans. Each healer walked her a little farther into the realm of Spirit, and each experience she had helped to reshape and define her new (and unlimited) reality a little more. The cold, rigid, small world she had formerly lived in gave way to what she described as "a trip better than the one my family took to Disneyland when John was alive."

When I asked her to explain in greater depth what she was discovering, she said, "I'm discovering that it's absolutely true we are unlimited spiritual beings. I haven't fully gotten my head wrapped around that fact quite yet, but when I'm not in my head, I know it's valid. I feel my Spirit; and it feels as if I'm the brightest, most beautiful light on the planet. I love me. I love others. I love life, and I'm no longer afraid. It's crazy to try to explain my experience because there aren't many words that can really describe what I'm discovering. Words somehow seem inadequate.

"The wild thing is I've never felt more alive, yet I would have never reached this expanded realm had John not died. We were both missing it completely. I realize now that his passing was—after my grief lifted—the greatest gift he ever gave both me and the kids. And now we thank him every day. I finally understand the line from the Bible: 'He died so that we may live.' It's true in our lives. Today we are really living, and before that we were merely existing."

Making the Shift

In the transformation process, everything that holds us back or no longer serves the purpose of our soul's growth dies off. We all undergo emotional, intellectual, and, ultimately, physical death as we are born to the unlimited experience of embracing our Divine nature.

These mini-deaths are frightening and tragic to the ego, but liberating to the Spirit. Just as a caterpillar must first release its old form before it can transform into the emancipated butterfly, life as we know it must also "die" in one form before it reappears in its newly liberated, Divine state.

Asking the Questions

Now take out your journal and turn your attention inward. Contemplate each of the following questions, and invite your Spirit, your most authentic self, to respond to each one. Give yourself plenty of time to feel the genuine response coming from your heart, the source of your power.

- What in your life feels as if it is dying?

- Do you want certain parts of your life to die? Are you allowing or trusting this end to come?

- Where do you feel most limited? What are you outgrowing?

- Is something new coming in? What is trying to get your attention and teach you something? Are you refusing to open up to it?

- Who or what has died, leaving you to reevaluate your ideas and beliefs about life?

- In what ways has that death or ending opened you up to a new beginning?

- Is your Spirit alive, or does it feel as if your kefi has gone missing?

- How might you better resuscitate your Spirit and give it new life? (Really take your time on this question and allow your Spirit to answer. It will guide you if you let it.)

After writing down your answers, set aside your journal and remain seated. Close your eyes, and calmly breathe in and out through your nose. Start with a sigh or two to help you relax. Think of a time when you let go of an old belief and opened yourself up to a new understanding.

With your next breath, let all of your tension go and simply *be* for a moment or two, even longer if possible. Enjoy sitting and breathing deeply, empty of all thought, free of any agenda, and in the moment. Feel this vibration of being connected to Source. Notice how peaceful, content, and even energized you feel. This is the power of your Spirit, and it's available to you at all times. It is the real you. *Remember this.*

Daily Practice: Let Go

When transforming into Divine eternal beings, we learn to no longer attach ourselves as deeply or strongly to the physical plane or to other individuals. Likewise, we should not blindly hold on to particular ideas, beliefs, or attitudes. Following the numerous examples in nature—such as the caterpillar's transformation to a butterfly—willingly release any attachment that causes unnecessary struggle, and allow new energy and solutions to come in. What in your life should you release today? Can you let it go?

This can be an attachment to a person, an outworn attitude, or a limiting belief about someone or something (including yourself). It could be an attachment through fear to an unhappy work situation, a negative judgment about yourself or someone else, or even the need to always get your own way.

If you aren't sure what you should release at this moment, don't worry; you'll know soon enough. Look for conflict. Wherever there is conflict, there's an opportunity to release your ego a little more, and in doing so, you open up and allow your Spirit to take over. Your work is to be *willing* to let go of the ego's perspective and allow a higher one to come in every day, in every situation of your life. The more challenging this is, the greater the invitation to do so. To hold on to a position, belief, opinion, or conflict in the name of righteousness blocks your Spirit. Remember, all that dies returns in a higher form.

> *"And the day came when the risk to remain tight in the bud was more painful than the risk it took to blossom."*
>
> — ANAÏS NIN

The Virtual Healing Tour

Eileen was never a confident person. She tried to build her self-esteem, but not very hard. She did her work each day, but never with two feet fully in. She showed up and took care of her responsibilities, but just enough to get by.

It was always that way with her, and she didn't consider it a problem. She was an average student in school, making it through college with the minimum passing grades, and immediately went into the hospitality business after graduating. She started as a waitress in the dining room of a beautiful hotel, and eventually worked her way up to the banquet department and ran special events. Her path was gradual and steady, advancing one slow step at a time; and while she did her job well enough to keep it, she never felt that it was her passion. She just did as she was told and kept moving along.

One thing she did enjoy in the hospitality industry, however, was the never-ending parade of interesting people, some of whose backgrounds and philosophies in life differed greatly from her own. One of those guests was Louise Hay, considered by many as the leader of the New Thought movement. Louise was staying at the hotel while in town to give a talk, and Eileen waited on her in the restaurant. Their brief, friendly conversation led Eileen to attend Louise's lecture that evening, where she was introduced to the world of spirituality and metaphysics for the first time. From the moment she took home a signed copy of Louise's book *You Can Heal Your Life*, Eileen was hooked.

She couldn't get enough and began to consume metaphysical and spiritual books similar to, as she described it, "a kid hooked on sugar." She spent hours in the spiritual section of bookstores on her days off and bought every newly released title that came out on the subject. It wasn't unusual for her to buy three or four books at a time, not to mention those she ordered online or from the many spiritually minded book clubs she'd joined along the way. Eventually, weeks of doing this turned into many years.

Eileen, voracious reader that she now was, soon became an expert on meditation, knowing every type there was, including mindful meditation, walking meditation, yoga meditation, eating meditation, and everything else in between. She learned the importance of being in the moment, the meaning of "Be here now," and the waste of living in the past or future. She was introduced to the third dimension, the fourth dimension, and the fifth! She read all about angels, Spirit guides, light beings, ascended masters, and even aliens. Ultimately, she believed that everything she read was vastly more interesting than the world she lived in.

Eileen's discovery process eventually led her into the realm of manifestation, where she was introduced to the power of intention as a way to realize one's dreams— messages she found in my books *Your Heart's Desire* and *The Answer Is Simple.* The latter attracted her because of the title. She'd read so much over the years that everything had become overwhelmingly complicated. She didn't know what to believe or who to follow; and she wanted to be sure that she didn't make a mistake. So the notion that the answer could actually be simple was very appealing.

Over the years, Eileen accumulated so many spiritual books that she could have opened her own bookstore. She loved what she read, especially when she felt tired, unappreciated, depressed, and most of all, insecure. The words soothed her. She went to work every day as expected, but she didn't feel secure in her job and constantly worried that her boss would fire her at any moment. Her books helped her cope with such disturbing thoughts, so she raced home to them night after night at the end of a long day of work. It was how she released her anxiety.

Eileen must have learned something about manifesting because she actually did get fired after 20 years on the job, yet none of her books could change that reality. She couldn't say it caught her by surprise, because she'd had several run-ins with the newly hired manager of the hotel over the past few months. He wasn't satisfied with her halfhearted performance and repeatedly warned her to improve. So when the day arrived that she received a pink slip, she realized she'd been expecting it. Secretly, she knew that her manager had a valid point. She hadn't gone the distance, and he was the first person in her life to call her on it. Nevertheless, she was so hurt, lost, and ashamed that she withdrew from the world and buried herself even deeper in her reading. She let her husband take care of her and refused to find a new job.

In spite of the countless books Eileen read over the past two decades, she felt completely lost. She couldn't find her Spirit anywhere and hadn't a clue as to where to look next. That's when it became painfully obvious to her that an intellectual pursuit of the Spirit wasn't enough to empower a person. Sure, she could recite myriad teachings as if she were an expert, but she hadn't followed through with a single practice (and if she had, she did it with the same halfhearted effort as everything else she attempted in life).

It was as if she'd read a million manuals on how to ride a bike but never actually sat on one and started pedaling. Her spiritual journey was a virtual one—the ideas appealing, yet untested and unpracticed in her life. There were no tangible results. Eileen's discovery process had deteriorated into spiritual window-shopping— gazing upon but not actually attaining any of the positive benefits. In the end, she realized that she was no better off than those who were clueless about their Spirit. Perhaps she was even worse off, because although she knew the power that was there for her, she couldn't get to it.

Eileen's plight is very common. I know a lot of "spiritual junkies" who could put me to shame with all they know about the spiritual realm. There are those who could pass as scholars, yet haven't ever applied even one simple spiritual practice they've learned on a regular basis. They remain stuck in their minds, closed off in their hearts, and painfully cut off from the true joy and power of Spirit. They are lost in the land of "virtual discovery" and cannot seem to find their way out. This is because, as Eileen was so acutely reminded, learning involves far more than gathering information or memorizing facts. To really learn something, one must apply the information regularly enough to experience it directly. Eileen admitted that every time she decided to start a new practice, she would do it for a day or so, but soon enough, she'd get frustrated and give up—going back to doing what she had always done without taking any responsibility for her transformation.

"My spiritual books were a way to hide from life," she courageously stated after our last conversation. "I could talk the talk so well that no one really asked me to walk the walk. So I didn't! Truthfully, I didn't want to. It took too much effort to change. I didn't want to be that responsible for my life. I wanted to just show up and have others take care of me. And honestly, my way worked up to a point. I showed up for work, and my employer took care of me. I showed up to my marriage, and my husband took care of me. What I hadn't 'shown up' for, however, is *myself;* and now nothing is taking care of me. Not even my spiritual books."

I suggested that Eileen take her discovery process to a whole new level and give all of her books away, except for ten, at the most. As she herself admitted, her books were a way for her to escape and tune out the world, rather than tune in to her Spirit. At first she balked, almost like a junkie being asked to give up her stash, but eventually she relented, saying: "I know you're right.

These books are keeping me from actually making any real change in my life. I've been making the mistake of thinking that just because I've read something, I know it and it becomes true in my life, but that's not the case. It's time to put to practice what I've learned."

As a messenger of spiritual teachings, I know that books have their place. That's why I write them. They get the message across, but they don't offer a detour to real learning. They're the manuals to *assist* in one's learning. The real lessons come from firsthand experience. I suggested that rather than read any more books, Eileen should offer an introductory course on spiritual meditation to her friends.

"We teach best what we're here to learn," I shared with her. "It might feel scary putting together even a simple two-hour course on meditation, but it will make you commit enough to it yourself to convince others to try it."

"But how could I ever do that if I've never really meditated?" she gasped, horrified by my suggestion.

"There's only one way," I answered. "Prepare for the course by actually meditating. Then you can share your authentic experience—all of it. That's learning, and others will benefit from what you share."

At first Eileen laughed, but I knew she was intrigued. She certainly knew enough people who might want to attend such a course. She talked so often about what she'd read that it wouldn't seem odd for her to do such a thing.

I don't know if Eileen followed through or not. I do know, however, that she was ready to have a real discovery process—not just a virtual one. The Universe was asking more of her, and if she didn't genuinely shift, she knew she would be left behind.

"Who knows?" she said, both laughing and sounding relieved as we prepared to hang up the phone. "Maybe my Spirit got me fired so I'd stop faking in front of myself and everyone else. At least now I have to get real, because there's no one to rescue me. My husband is fed up with me, I lost my job because my boss was fed up with me, and now *I'm* fed up with me. I'm ready for a *real* change, and I know it begins with me."

"So let the discovery begin," I told her. "At least now you've got nothing to lose."

Making the Shift

Discovering your Spirit is tremendously exciting and liberating. And yet, to simply hear about doing so isn't the same thing. Friends can tell you all about their wonderful trip to Europe, for example, complete with a video documentary and souvenirs, but you won't really discover Europe until you actually go there yourself.

The same holds true for the realm of Spirit. You won't really know the power of your Spirit until you connect with it directly through meditation, mindful and conscious awareness of your negative ego patterns, conscious breathing to break out of those patterns, and the decision to tune in to your Spirit every day.

To genuinely discover your Spirit, stop talking, stop reading, and start listening to your heart. Be silent long enough to feel your Divine self within. There is no other way to truly live.

Asking the Questions

Now take out your journal and turn your attention inward. Contemplate each of the following questions, and invite your Spirit, your most authentic self, to respond to each one. Give yourself plenty of time to feel the genuine response coming from your heart, the source of your power.

- What do you want to explore but haven't done yet? Why not? Is there something you're aware of in your heart but haven't yet embraced or acted upon?

- Is there any subject you consider yourself to be an expert in and feel that there's nothing else you need to learn?

- Are you in the habit of listening to your heart? When and how do you do this?

- When seeking guidance, do you ask others for their opinion, or do you go inward and ask your authentic self—your Spirit?

- Does someone else's opinion override the inner voice of your Spirit?

- Have you spent much time reading spiritual books before this one? If so, did you incorporate certain suggestions or recommendations you learned into your life? How much effort did you put forth?

- How committed are you to being connected with your Spirit? Would you say you are just curious or perhaps very committed?

- What are you willing to do to discover the power of your Spirit? Do you plan to just try a few things and see what happens, or are you willing to do whatever it takes?

- Are you hiding your authentic self? In what ways?

After writing down your answers, set aside your journal and remain seated. Close your eyes, and calmly breathe in and out through your nose. Start with a sigh or two to help you relax. Tell yourself that you will no longer put aside the need to connect with your Spirit, your authentic self. Feel the power of your own Divine creative spark.

With your next breath, let all of your tension go and simply *be* for a moment or two, even longer if possible. Enjoy sitting and breathing deeply, empty of all thought, free of any agenda, and in the moment. Feel this vibration of being connected to Source. Notice how peaceful, content, and even energized you feel. This is the power of your Spirit, and it's available to you at all times. It is the real you. *Remember this.*

Daily Practice: Be Silent

Take a few moments every day to sit in silence and turn your full awareness inward to connect with your Spirit. It can be a moment in the shower or just after parking your car. It can be as you wash your hands before dinner or while you wait for the train on your way home from work. It can be while folding laundry or watering your plants. These moments of silence can occur anytime and anyplace. The more you learn to tune in wherever you are, the easier it will become.

There's no need to focus on any particular thing as you do so. Simply listen to your inner voice, much like you would listen to a person speaking to you on the phone. Just give that voice your full attention.

It may take a moment or two for the mental chatter of your ego to quiet down so you can hear. Be patient because *it* will. Relax as you listen. Your Spirit has powerful guidance to offer, so give it your full attention at least for a few minutes. Be aware of any intuitive hits, bright ideas, flashes, or creative thoughts that may cross your mind. They will arise quickly and leave just as quickly, so it's important to be aware of their subtlety. You may hear them in your mind; or you might feel, sense, see, or simply notice them. Or all of the above!

Get used to noticing these subtle flashes of insight and intuition, in whatever guise they appear. One effective way to do so is to speak them out loud as they appear in your mind so that you capture them before they slip away. Once you vocalize your heart-centered awareness, you don't have to do anything else. Just feel your feelings, letting them sink in. Allow them to visit you without chasing them away or having to justify themselves. Simply get the feel for your Spirit and how it communicates with you.

Spirit can be best felt in silence. If you pay close attention, you can actually distinguish the feeling of intuition and Spirit from that of your ego-based intelligence. Spirit leaves you feeling expanded, peaceful, surprised, and inspired; you're left with an open heart and mind. Ego, on the other hand, leaves you feeling tense and contracted; you're left with a closed or defensive heart and mind.

The more you practice sitting in silence for a few short moments, the more quickly you can intercept these often highly subtle outreaches from your Spirit. When silent, you feel the inner vibration of Spirit in your heart. It's warm yet powerful; strong yet kind. It is direct, always unconditionally loving. The more you feel it, the more you will recognize it, and the more you will be moved by it.

"We need to find God, and he cannot be found in noise and restlessness. God is the friend of silence."

— MOTHER TERESA

Discovering your Spirit is like suddenly entering a magical land where anything is possible. Just like when you were a student, you've picked up all of your "school supplies" and are ready for the first day of class. But even though you're well prepared for change through the discovery process, remember that until you practice what you've been taught, until you've incorporated it into your life, real learning has yet to take place. But once you commit yourself, you'll be ready for the next stage in transformation: surrendering your ego and personal will over to your Divine Spirit.

This can be especially challenging, as it asks you to make the first real shifts in how you move through life. Even though you're awake and aware—acknowledging that it's the best force to follow in life—you must still make the actual choice to trust your Spirit over your fears . . . and that can feel quite scary. After all, although you've struggled with life and want a change, you're still entering the unknown and there are no guarantees. The next stage fortunately passes rather quickly. Like jumping off a diving board, the fear and hesitation you feel beforehand is forgotten and replaced by elation once you make the leap. The same holds true for surrendering into your Spirit. You'll feel excited and joyful, immediately sensing the return of your kefi, once you begin to release control to your higher Divine Spirit.

Before we dive into the next stage, I want to share a beautiful, creative (and very effective) way to help you anchor your life in Spirit every day so that surrendering your ego becomes easier while your connection to your authentic Divine self grows stronger.

Chapter Four

CREATING YOUR PERSONAL ALTAR

To genuinely feel the power of Spirit, you must make it a central part of your life—something you want to connect with automatically without pause or hesitation. One way to help you achieve this is by creating a personal altar in your home and sitting quietly in front of it every day for a few minutes (preferably during peaceful moments in the morning). Make it a daily ritual so that you can connect with the Holy Spirit within before you enter the outside world and begin your day.

There is no right or wrong way to set up an altar—just follow your inner guidance. What you do create should reflect your personal energetic field. An altar is meant to be a visual reminder for you to go within through prayer, meditation, contemplation, song, or intuitive listening. You set an intention to detach from the outer world of ego-oriented power and shift internally to an elevated dimension of love in your heart. Your altar serves as an anchor for you to practice setting your personal vibration so that it resonates with the flow of Divine Source.

An altar is more than a beautiful "thing" to look at. It connects you to your Spirit in profound ways. Sitting at your altar trains your conscious and subconscious mind to change familiar ego patterns (which have habitually controlled you) and open you up to a more loving, authentic frequency of Spirit. Keep in mind that you're guiding your ego to let go and surrender to a higher power.

Altars also serve as energetic portals, or openings, to Spirit. When you enter this sacred energy, the veil between the worlds thins, and the heavens open up. If you hold the intention of connecting to your Spirit, you'll be "spirited away" into a beautiful higher realm. At first, it may be so subtle that you hardly notice the changes through your senses, but with repeated visits, your perception of this heightened vibrational pattern becomes stronger. And no matter what you may be thinking about when approaching your altar, your mind will quickly become calm, quiet, and clear; and your heart will open as your vibration elevates to one of pure loving-kindness.

With daily practice, you'll actually *feel* this sacred opening to the Spirit realm as you approach your altar; it's the same as what you might experience when you approach an altar in a church or other holy place. If you haven't felt this or don't think you're energetically sensitive, be patient. Sitting for a few minutes each day in the energy of your personal altar will sharpen your perception.

The shift in vibration around your altar is created by regular, intentional acts of meditation, prayer, song, chant, and contemplation. If there's no holy inner work going on, though, the vibration of Spirit won't be present; and the portal won't open. It will simply be something pretty to look at, but it won't possess Divine life force. Therefore, I encourage you to create your altar with holy intention, reverence, and enthusiasm. It's up to you to open the door to subtle realms so that you can feel the loving support and renewal of your Spirit.

Some people have questioned whether creating an altar makes a real difference or if it's just for those who are trying to look and feel spiritual when they really don't feel anything at all. My response is that long ago before formal religion took over spirituality, practically everyone had an altar at home. Connecting to a Divine Source was a very intimate experience. In ancient times, men and women lived in constant dialogue with their Great Creator, and this connection wasn't taken for granted.

We started becoming disconnected when our altars were moved out of our homes and into the churches. Bit by bit, we became more removed from an intimate relationship with Divine Spirit, as we were taught to go through intermediaries such as priests and other clergy members in order to connect. Soon enough, and not surprisingly, our personal sensitivity to a higher vibration became obscured and was further diminished by the guilt and shame that was also drilled into us by many religious leaders. This caused us to totally disconnect from our link to Spirit and our Divine Creator, because we were made to feel unworthy. We must remove these dark clouds and reactivate our awareness of Spirit once again.

One of the most powerful ways to do so is by setting up a beautiful altar that reflects what is sacred to *you*.

Converse with God, or Source, in this sacred portal; and you'll begin to heal your wounded heart, opening up once again to your authentic self and Spirit.

Where to Place Your Altar

Making room in your home for an altar might not seem like the easiest thing to do, especially if you live in tight quarters, but with a little creativity, it's not difficult. Set up your altar in a room that's not used every day, such as a spare bedroom or dining room, or simply clear a small area in any room. A personal altar doesn't require a lot of space—that's not the point. It can be one square foot in size and still open up a tremendous portal if it was created by your heartfelt devotion, love, and intention to connect to your Spirit.

My personal altar is in my bedroom. I set it up on a small table in front of the window, and it's one of the first things I see every morning. I'm energetically drawn to it and always start my day there. It's a powerful living force, enabling me to become grounded and feel God's love. My husband, Patrick, created his own altar in his office; and it's set up on a tall, slim stand. His altar is very different from mine and reflects who he is, which is exactly what it should do. So know that you can certainly have more than one altar in your home. Each family member can set up his or her own unique space—and I believe that everyone should! It's an easy way to create a private, sacred portal between you and your Divine Spirit.

What to Place on Your Altar

What you put on your altar is of great importance, as each item vibrates with you and activates the power of your Spirit. Use whatever energetically resonates with you and touches your heart. For some people, this may mean including a picture of a spiritual figure, such as Mother Mary, Jesus, an Ascended Master Teacher, the Buddha, Krishna, Vishnu, Kali, or the Dalai Lama. Use images or things that really speak to you—those that you feel in your heart. That's the key to connecting to the power of your Spirit—*feeling.* So in addition to using images of holy or inspirational figures, also include photos of the people you love, such as your family and friends . . . and even photos of your pets can (and should) be placed on your altar.

Images and totems from nature may also resonate with you and activate the vibration of your Spirit. This may mean placing beautiful living things on your altar, such as fresh-cut flowers, fresh herbs and spices, or a bowl of clean water that's changed daily to symbolize the holy waters of Source. Your options are limitless.

Another way to elevate your vibration and connect with the power of your Spirit is by adding some natural crystals, especially quartz, to your altar. Often dismissed by more unconscious people as "silly New Age trinkets," crystals are extremely powerful living tools that can cut negative cords, remove unhealthy energetic attachments, clear energy fields, and even amplify personal intentions. They are essential in many fields today, including technology and medicine, for their power and precision; and they work with subtle realms of energy in profound ways.

That said, don't feel like you have to rush out and get one for your altar. On the other hand, don't be surprised if a beautiful crystal is suddenly attracted to you and finds its way into your life. You may see one in a store and feel drawn to it, or a friend may give you one as a gift. When something like this happens, it's a fun reminder of just how connected you are to Source. So be open, and see if your own special crystal comes your way soon.

Other wonderful objects to place on your altar are bird feathers, which also seem to somehow find their way to you. Feathers are totems of Spirit and represent the Divine self in flight. All living things, especially birds, intuit when someone is in the process of transformation or elevating his or her personal vibration. They support and affirm your growth and expansion of consciousness by sending you their feathers.

Since you're creating an active portal, bells, chimes, and rattles are other powerful objects to place on your altar to elevate your vibration and even help expand the portal's opening. Sacred hand drums are also potent for connecting with Source. Using these items actually calls your Spirit forward, which is why they have been incorporated in almost all religious practices throughout the ages to bring forth the Divine Spirit.

This is very personal, but I wanted to share something else about my own altar. I like to place a bit of chocolate on mine to remind me to never forget the sweetness of life, no matter how it's unfolding at any given moment. Many ancient religions viewed this delicacy as holy, and treasured it for its richness and soothing qualities. I put a piece of good dark chocolate on my altar as an offering to the Divine Spirit in gratitude for all the sweetness that Source has showered upon me throughout my life. Someone once asked me if I eventually eat the chocolate, but I never do . . . yet interestingly, it always seems to mysteriously disappear.

Beyond these examples, feel free to place anything else on your altar that speaks to your Spirit. Remember to select meaningful items to activate the portal to the subtle realms, while also opening your heart to Source energy in gratitude and appreciation for your life.

Approaching Your Altar

Approach the altar as if you were entering a doorway into a sacred space in which you will shift out of ordinary consciousness and into the subtle realm where your Divine Spirit will meet with Source.

A ritual to signify this shift of awareness is a very helpful clue for the conscious mind to step aside and allow the fullness of your Divine Spirit to come forward and merge with Source. This may be as simple as lighting a candle or a stick of incense on the altar, or ringing a small bell. As this is your experience and your connection, it's up to you to decide which ritual you want to engage in to activate the sacred portal you are about to enter.

I have a client, for instance, who washes her hands and face before she approaches her altar. To her, this symbolizes the purity of her Spirit as she temporarily leaves the physical world behind. Another client plays beautiful music beforehand; and yet another simply greets her altar each morning with a hearty "Hello, Father! Hello, Mother!" The ritual is yours to create as part of reclaiming the power of Spirit within you. Do what *feels* right to you. Sometimes you might want to approach your altar one way, and on another day, your feelings and entire ritual may change. That's okay; it's how Spirit works. It is the living, breathing, holy essence within you—it's *not* a static or fixed thing. Your Spirit is always ready to communicate with you, so think of this step as a way to open the conversation.

◎ ◎

Your personal altar serves as a powerful symbol for the real altar where you meet with Spirit in your heart space. Envision this as the holy foundation of your life—an opening into the unlimited, Divine expanse of the Universe. Don't force this awareness. Simply allow and imagine it to be so. Take your time, and let whatever thoughts or feelings float freely into your mind. Sit in this space for as long as you can. You should do this for at least a few minutes every day. If you have more time, sit longer. Be aware of your breathing, keeping it easy and relaxed. Make sure you don't hold your breath.

If you feel inclined to pray, do so. If you want to sing, chant, or recite mantras, that's fine, too. If you wish to simply sit and relax, or ask questions, go for it. (If you aren't self-conscious, ask your questions out loud.)

Sitting at an altar and entering your heart space daily is the best way to experience the power of your Spirit. Creating an outer altar as a means of entering your inner one enables a holy, energetic shift in your life. It's not something that can be recognized by the intellect, so ignore your ego if it tries to analyze what's going on or dismiss your experience as if nothing real is happening.

Connecting to Spirit occurs through dedicated intention, prayer, awareness, meditation, and imagination. With repetition, it becomes your natural state of being. Take the time to create and connect with your Spirit at your altar, both outwardly and inwardly. This will help you maintain a strong connection to your Divine authentic self.

Harnessing the Power of the Six Directions

One way to train your awareness on the power of your Spirit is to recognize that you're bathing in a sea of spiritual energy. The more aware you are of this energy, the more quickly you will experience your transformation from a dense, physical consciousness to a subtler, elevated spiritual consciousness.

Stand before your altar and visualize yourself floating in the center of an energetic cube in space. See yourself surrounded by the energies and elements of the six directions: north, south, east, west, above, and below. Notice that each intersects at a middle point in the center of your heart. They all possess a particular vibration, a unique energetic frequency—a living force, or Spirit— that, if invited and invoked, offers healing and gifts that you can receive in your heart.

Working with the Divine forces of the six directions as you sit at your altar will quickly elevate your sensitivity to the power of your Spirit. For the remainder of this chapter, I'll describe how to connect to the Spirits of the six directions as my teachers and guides have taught me. Please note that this process may or may not resonate with you, and it shouldn't be considered as the right or only way. I'm just sharing with you what works for me at the moment. I may grow and change over time, and as I do, so will the rituals and techniques that I practice each day.

If you already have a regular routine or process that works for you, please continue to use it. If you have a religious practice that feels right to you, please use that. In other words, follow your Spirit, which is the entire point of creating an altar in the first place. Guard against the temptation to believe that there is only one right way to connect to your Divine self. That kind of thinking is merely a perpetuation of the patriarchal tradition of surrendering power to outside sources.

It's highly likely that in the beginning—especially if this is a new practice—you may feel very little or nothing at all. Don't let that frustrate you. In working with an altar, you are awakening the more subtle realms of your consciousness, which may be barely noticeable at first. Believe that your Spirit exists and will connect with you, and it will happen. You determine the rate of progress by your own level of consistency and devotion.

I suggest that you make this entire project— creating and sitting at your altar—something you truly love and enjoy. At the very least, your altar is a place where you can quiet your thoughts and meditate. At best, your heart will open, and you'll experience a profound connection with your Spirit that will alter your life completely.

Now let's move on to some of my suggestions for working with the energies of the six directions of Spirit.

East

Start by moving your altar so that you're facing eastward as you approach it. If this isn't possible, once you're sitting at your altar, simply turn your body to the east. Focus on this direction, and ask your imagination to feel its Spirit. The most powerful energy associated with this is, of course, the rising sun. See the sunrise in your mind's eye and feel the vibration it carries with it. If possible, sit at your altar, even if only on occasion, as the sun is rising so that you can connect with the greatest Source of life-force energy for the planet.

The vibration of the east energizes your Spirit with new ideas, inspiration, creative insight, innovation, and opportunities for a fresh start. Turn to the east for these energies to touch, influence, and feed your Spirit. Intuitively wonder in what ways your Spirit wants to move into new directions, and allow the frequency and vibration of the east to inform you.

Go even further and appeal to the Spirit of the east if you feel that you need a burst of vitality or an infusion of new experiences. Ask for exciting opportunities or experiences if you're in a rut, at a dead end, or at a point in life where you feel uninspired. Then allow yourself to embrace the energetic influence of the east as it touches your heart in service to your Spirit.

West

Next, place your attention to the Spirit of the west. Feel the energy, frequency, and vibration of what is now behind you; and turn around to face it. Imagine the setting sun in your mind's eye as you connect to this powerful living force. Focus on its desire to serve you by pulling away energies, activities, or circumstances that no longer serve you or have value in your life. The energy of the west attracts all stagnant, dead, or useless vibrations from your energetic field and returns them back to Source. It also assists in releasing grief and sadness, as these emotions must also eventually be surrendered to the natural flow of life.

Stop thinking and allow yourself to feel the force of the living Spirit of the west. What does it want to pull from you? What in your life needs to be finished or completed? In what ways do you need to move on and become present in your life? Don't allow your intellect to govern this exploration, as it resides in the left hemisphere and can't feel the Spirit of life. That can only be experienced in the right brain, where imagination and wonder rule. Engage this part of your brain as you invoke the Spirit of the west to remove all blocks so that you can continue to expand your full authentic expression in the natural flow of life.

North

Next, slowly and with deep breaths and awareness, turn your body and attention to the Spirit of the north. Open yourself up to its powerful influence. Notice how completely different in feeling and tone this frequency is from that of the east and west, each a living conscious force in your life. The energy of the north brings on a cold snap. It spurs you into action and helps get you moving in the direction of your authentic self.

The energies of the north guide you forward in life. This vibration and frequency reveals your next step—your next creation. It keeps you in the flow and serves as a star of possibility for you to reach toward. This is the Spirit of your dreams, your desires, and your intentions. The Spirit of the north reflects back to you who you are naturally designed to be, as the oak tree reflects the potential of the budding acorn. This energy resonates in your heart to keep you in touch with your soul, which is aching to give birth to greater expression. This powerful force keeps you faithful to your truth, vision, and heart song.

Invoke the Spirit of the north whenever you feel that you've lost your way. Call upon it when you doubt yourself or feel out of touch with your passion. Allow the Spirit to touch your heart and pull you back to center—into the flow and aligned with your authentic self. Let this powerful energy ignite your inner fire and keep you moving forward.

South

The Spirit of the south is like a dark cave, symbolizing mystery, wonder, and depth. The Spirit of kindness, rest, and recuperation, it represents the time for meditation, dreaming, and even slumber. The powerful energy of the south embodies inner knowing and calls upon you to remember who you are. It guides you away from the immediate outer circumstances and leads you into the peaceful, darkened cave within—to a place where thought ceases, feelings quiet, and ancient wisdom speaks.

Invoke the Spirit of the south when you know it's time to dive deeper into your human journey and capture the more profound meaning of your experiences. Allow its influence into your heart to help you feel greater awareness, understanding, and honesty toward yourself. This mysterious force offers you an invitation to return to authenticity. It is the Spirit of truth. Call upon the energy of the south when you've lost your connection with your true self and no longer feel your path under your feet. Allow this Spirit to return you to self and reawaken your soul. Seek its power when peace is what you need.

Above

Maintain your focus, and turn your attention to the space above you. Feel the Spirit of the heavens as you connect with the light above and the stars in the sky. Draw on the power of the subtle Divine beings as they rain their support and wisdom into your crown, the highest point of your head, guiding you on the walk of life.

The Spirit of the heavens provides companionship, assistance, healing, support, direction, confirmation, and assurance. Make contact with the heavens to chart your course, stay on the path, and rise to new dimensions. Listen to their subtle messages—felt in the twinkle of a star, the shifting of the clouds, the hum in your ears, and the love all around you. Open your awareness and ask the Spirit above to lead the way and keep you true to yourself throughout your journey.

This realm is the playground of the star beings, Spirit healers, light beings, angels, and ascended masters. Access their wisdom by directing your attention to the heavens. Feel their presence, and follow their loving guidance.

Below

Continuing to access the Divine flow of all directions, now turn your attention to the Spirit of the earth. Feel the Great Mother, Gaia, the Divine gorgeous being that provides the solid foundation beneath your feet. Feel her in your bones, as your physical body is made from her. Open your eyes and heart space, and let her power in. Sense her royalty in nature all around you. Recognize her as a living Spirit, the most magnificent in the human experience.

Allow your awareness to go deep into the earth. A giant magnetic force is at the center of her core, pulling and keeping the form of the planet together. Feel this pull on your heart.

Focus your attention on the layers of bones buried in her fields, carrying the presence of your ancestors, as well as all those who have walked the earth before you. Acknowledge that their bones have turned to the dust that now becomes the rich soil for new life and new growth. Tune in to the full awareness of her gifts, shared with you in every way. Breathe in her Spirit, and be humble before her greatness.

Reaching the Heart Space

Standing in front of your altar, now bring your full awareness and attention inward, to the very center of your heart. This is sacred space, a portal that opens to the unlimited, holy you. It is the point where the Spirits of all six directions converge and commune, coming to this particular point to create your unique experience.

This is where you leave the three-dimensional world of ego and experience your unlimited, authentic spiritual self. In the heart space, you cease to be contained by time or space, by your history or family, or by past or present circumstances. All this fades away. It is your experience, but not your true self.

Through breathing, focus your attention on journeying even deeper into your heart space. With each breath in, envision going around and around just as if you were a stream of water swirling down a drain. With your inner eye, watch your awareness travel in this manner until it finally drops into the very center of your heart and opens into an infinite, unlimited world on the other side.

Don't worry if this expanded sense of being doesn't occur the first time you try to enter your heart space. Simply focus on the center of your heart and let yourself experience whatever awareness comes about. Sit quietly in that space for a few minutes, remembering to relax, breathe, and listen.

◎ ◎

If you spend time at your altar every day as part of your spiritual practice, you'll establish such a powerful connection to your Spirit that you'll actually be able to feel its higher, more peaceful vibration. The beautiful energy you create when you're meditating there draws you into your Spirit gently and easily.

You'll soon find yourself looking forward to sitting at your altar. Since it serves as your convenient meeting place with Spirit, maintaining contact with your Divine authentic self no longer seems so challenging.

You have successfully begun the journey through the first two stages, awakening to and slowly discovering your Spirit. You're putting forth the effort by incorporating what you're learning into your daily life. Thus, the creation of your own altar has acted as a natural springboard to the third stage of your transformation: *surrendering* to your Spirit.

Chapter Five

STAGE THREE: SURRENDERING TO YOUR SPIRIT

The third stage of transformation is to surrender to your Spirit. This means moving beyond the parameters and perceived safety of your ego and turning your well-being over to the mysterious, unlimited realm of intuition. This allows the Holy Spirit within to move you, make your decisions, establish your values and priorities, and take direct action in your life.

Surrendering to your Spirit indicates that you finally recognize that your ego has highly limited, if any, real power, and is preventing you from feeling at peace or realizing your potential. While the discovery stage is essential to the transformation process, until you surrender to your Spirit and allow it to take over your life, what you've learned won't make any difference. You'll remain trapped in the world of illusion, struggling to stay a step ahead of your fears.

When you're ready to surrender, you're ready to put to use what you've learned in the discovery phase and let your Spirit move you through life. Surrendering to your Spirit may be too great to fathom at first, and it can feel as if you're being asked to take a crazy leap into the abyss. It is a leap . . . but not into the abyss. You're stepping into the flow of life and the full support of the Universe. When you surrender, you come to realize that what you know is not *all* there is to know, what you perceive is not necessarily an accurate view of the world, and what you think is possible is not *all* that is truly possible. So you open to the Universe to help you—to show you another, better way to live.

For some, this stage feels like death to the ego. It isn't. Rather, it's more like a demotion. As I've said earlier, the ego by itself isn't really the problem for most people. However, depending on the ego to do a job that it's inherently not equipped and qualified to do is the *real* problem. The ego is a biased, limited apparatus that finds solutions from a defensive and distorted point of view, generally leading you down the wrong road. The Holy Spirit, on the other hand, allows you direct access to the quantum field of all possibility. It is through your Spirit that the most loving solutions, inspired insights, and profound personal healings are revealed. To surrender means to let go, get out of your own way, and have faith. This becomes easier when you fall into greater alignment with your most authentic nature as a Divine being. The minute you connect with your genuine self, trusting the Universe stops feeling threatening and starts feeling natural.

Rarely does surrendering to your Spirit happen with a single decision, moment, or event. Even if you fully choose to release control, you still have to break the habit of living from the ego mind-set as you've been taught. To surrender to Source as a Divine being takes consistent practice and intention. Remember that the ego doesn't give up its power easily and will most likely put up a fight.

Realistically, this process happens in stages, one day at a time, as you begin to break the habit of solely looking to your rational mind for guidance. Consciously surrendering every day is the only way to fully transform. It may take weeks, months, or even years before your ego truly gives up and trusts in Source. Yet once that occurs, life becomes miraculous.

The invitation to decrease the ego's hold presents itself in many ways, both small and large, throughout each day. But every time you surrender, the outcome is so positive, so surprising, and so much better than your ego could have ever created on its own that before you know it, it becomes obvious that aligning with your Spirit is the only sane way to live. Any effort you make—every struggle you face and overcome—will always pay off. Spirit heals everyone and everything, every time.

Surrendering to Spirit is inevitable for all of us in this great transformational cycle on Earth. In the end, we must accept our Divine essence and draw from our Spirit. This may take years, or possibly even lifetimes. Those who refuse for whatever reason will eventually have to admit that their way doesn't work. Like a battery running out of power, unless we connect to a Source, our limited personal energy dwindles and dies. We all come to realize the limitations of the ego, because that is the purpose of the soul's journey on Earth.

The level of difficulty for your transition is up to *you*. Your ability to release control can comprise constant allowing or intense battling. Either way, your ego will never prevail over your Spirit.

Playing the Tabla

I have a friend named Ben who is a wonderful drummer and has been playing for more than 20 years. He said his skills just came naturally to him and required no real thought or awareness on his part. He just feels the music and bangs away to the rhythm. Over the years he's played with several bands, and his talent has increased, yet he's never recalled a time when he had to really focus or work at it. It's just what he did.

Then Ben went to India, where he experienced masterful Indian musicians playing an ancient type of drums called the tabla (a pair of hand drums that are of different sizes and produce different timbres), and he was so moved by the performance that it nearly brought him to tears. He was mesmerized and entered a deep trancelike state. It was unlike any other musical experience he'd ever had, either while playing or listening.

The tabla spoke to his soul and awoke something in him. It felt like coming home. Immediately, he knew he wanted to create that music for himself. So when Ben returned to Chicago, he bought a beautiful pair of tabla at a world-music store and sat down to play them as soon as he got home. However, no matter what he tried, he couldn't re-create the sounds that the Indian musicians had made. Every single thing he knew about drumming—every natural impulse, every technique he knew—completely failed to bring forth any semblance of music out of these strange drums. The way he was used to playing simply didn't work (and he could play many different types of percussion instruments).

For the first time, Ben couldn't wing it, nor could he fake it. He couldn't even teach himself to play these drums, as he'd done many times in the past. They seemed to have a different set of rules, and he had no idea what they were. He didn't know where to begin. The tabla spoke a completely foreign language.

Ben was shocked and frustrated by this unexpected barrier. He hadn't planned on this requiring much effort on his part, and he certainly didn't think the possibility existed that he wouldn't be able to play them at all.

He realized that if he wanted to play this instrument, he'd have to start all over. He would have to become a beginner, which meant unlearning everything he already knew about percussion. This challenged his ego significantly. He'd even have to find a teacher and make time to practice. But he was already so busy. It seemed like a lot more work than it was worth, so he walked away for a while and let the drums sit in the corner, silent.

After nine months of ignoring (or at least attempting to ignore) the tabla, Ben's ego quieted down enough for him to once again feel his Spirit urging him to play them. He knew that it was his ego stopping him from engaging in the experience that was calling to him now. He didn't want to be a beginner, a student. He certainly didn't want someone to show him how to do something that he already knew how to do. *I'm a good drummer,* he'd say to himself. *Why should I stress myself out trying to learn this? I won't use the tabla anyway. I have no place to play them. What's the point?* And so the conversation went in his head. Yet, as convincing as it was, it never felt true. His desire to play didn't go away; his ego just overwhelmed and silenced it.

Then one day after Ben enjoyed an unusually peaceful morning, he looked up from his computer and the tabla seemed to wink at him. It was as if it were trying to tell him something: *Come on, Ben. It's time to learn. Don't be afraid. Open your heart and mind, and enter the unknown.*

Suddenly, all of his excuses faded away. Something in him opened up. He felt ready! His ego was finally quiet, and he could hear the Spirit of the tabla calling to him, just as it had the first time he'd heard it in India. In that moment, he surrendered and said yes. He stopped avoiding what his heart yearned for, and instead decided to move toward it. What did he have to lose?

Ben found a great teacher—one of the best in the world, in fact—and began the arduous learning process. It has been going very slowly for him; and each lesson challenges his patience, dedication, and ego in every way. On some days, he must practice making a single sound, over and over again, for 45 minutes or more. Just one sound. His lessons require that he be mindful of everything he does with his hands and fingers, from where he places them on the drums to how hard he must flick his wrist to produce a particular tone, for instance. Nothing about this process is automatic, at least not yet. It takes great focus, awareness, and intention on his part to succeed in the tiniest way. There are still days when he wonders why he's bothering to do this.

But he *is* bothering. He's inspired by training his mind to work in new ways. And each victorious note he creates on the tabla, however small, feels like he just won a gold medal. Most of all, his effort brings his Spirit tremendous satisfaction. The more he surrenders his ego to his intention, the more vibrant and joyful he feels—not just about the tabla, but about every aspect of his life.

When he's practicing, Ben stops thinking and simply experiences the instrument. His mind becomes quiet. The past and future go away, and he feels timeless. His discipline rewards him with soul satisfaction, giving voice to his evolving Spirit. These kinds of benefits can't be measured in the physical, ego-based world.

Ben isn't able to play well enough for others yet, and he's a long way from being able to make money playing them at his current skill level. If anything, he'd be met with wrinkled brows and curious remarks. His effort is strictly personal, and the rewards are, too.

That is exactly why this process is so worthwhile. Ben is doing what his Spirit wants for him, not anyone else, and he is putting forth the discipline and effort it commands in spite of his ego-based objections. His ego doesn't want to relinquish its power, so it still constantly urges him to quit. Yet since he made the choice to act on his Spirit's desire, his ego's efforts to distract him have become weak and ineffectual, and surprisingly easy to ignore.

In following his Spirit, Ben is challenged *and* fed by his experience. When he's working on his daily lessons, he feels present and fully alive. The rest of the world fades away; all that remains is his intention, his Spirit, the Spirit of the tabla, and the Spirit of music. He is discovering that they're all expressions of the same thing, which is love. Without his concerted effort, he wouldn't have had this profound, expansive awareness of himself and life.

Making the Shift

Making the shift to an empowered, Spirit-based life takes attention, discipline, and practice. More often than not, what comes easily or even feels "natural" to you isn't in alignment with your authentic self. To shift from ego to Spirit requires a big change in your life—changing your priorities and values, how you spend your time, your inner dialogue, your focus, your availability to others, and your ability to surrender control. This is where the effort on your part comes in.

If you want to live in your empowered Spirit, be aware that it might be very different from the way you're accustomed to living. It will definitely require you to drop your present habits and create new ones. You know this is possible, but only by making a concerted effort to do so.

Consider this: Living from your Spirit is like learning to play an instrument, with all new rules for making music. The rules of the ego-based world for making music start with: "Live for others' approval." The Spirit-empowered rules start with: "Live for your own approval, and be willing to stand in the discomfort of others' disapproval." The ego-based rules continue with: "Don't change anything; it's dangerous." The Spirit-empowered rule is: "Embrace change. Welcome it. It's natural and healthy, and it brings growth." The ego-based rule is: "Be responsible, and do your duty. If what you're doing doesn't make money or serve a practical purpose, then it's a waste of time." The Spirit-empowered rule is: "If it calls to you, speaks to your creativity, brings out your most authentic self, honors your truth, opens your heart, and challenges you to grow, then it is the most important thing you can do in the world."

The ego wants things to be quick, predictable, and easy. If change is involved, the ego will do everything to stop it. To the ego, change means danger or even death. The rational mind relies on the past to guide it in the moment, and change signifies that the past doesn't apply now. The paradox is that once you begin to embrace change and become creatively inspired by it, your ego quiets down. It resists change until it is happening. Then the resistance stops, and your Spirit takes over.

Asking the Questions

Now take out your journal and turn your attention inward. Contemplate each of the following questions, and invite your Spirit, your most authentic self, to respond to each one. Give yourself plenty of time to feel the genuine response coming from your heart, the source of your power.

- What new creative expression or learning experience is calling to you? For example, playing a new instrument, taking voice lessons, signing up for a painting class, making time for a spiritual retreat, learning a new language, going rock climbing, enrolling in a digital-photography course, or writing poetry?

- How long have you felt this impulse or urging? A week, month, or even years? Where do you think this is coming from?

- Are you listening to this impulse and following it? If you are, what challenges has this brought up?

- What rewards are you experiencing by following your Spirit's impulse?

- How does it feel to open up to exploring new avenues, places, people, things, and even parts of your own nature?

- If you aren't following these impulses from Spirit, what are the reasons you give yourself for not doing so? Do they feel true?

- Are you afraid to change or upset things? What scares you the most?

- How does it feel to try to prevent things from changing? (Try to be as specific as possible.)

- How does your choice to say no to your inner Spirit leave you feeling? Energized? Constrained? (Again, be as specific as possible.)

- Do you wonder what saying yes to the urgings of your Spirit might do for you? Do you allow yourself to contemplate such things?

After writing down your answers, set aside your journal and remain seated. Close your eyes, and calmly breathe in and out through your nose. Start with a sigh or two to help you relax. Quiet your mind and listen. What is your Spirit urging or encouraging you to do? Are you willing to give it a try?

With your next breath, let all of your tension go and simply *be* for a moment or two, even longer if possible. Enjoy sitting and breathing deeply, empty of all thought, free of any agenda, and in the moment. Feel this vibration of being connected to Source. Notice how peaceful, content, and even energized you feel. This is the power of your Spirit, and it's available to you at all times. It is the real you. *Remember this.*

Daily Practice: Express Your Spirit

Choose to follow one creative impulse or urge arising from your Spirit every day. The simpler the better. It could be as basic as doodling on a sketch pad for 15 minutes every day, or as ambitious as signing up for a foreign-language class that meets regularly. Since this involves introducing something new into your life, trade it for one habit or practice that you do now but know is really of no value to your Spirit.

For example, your ego may be in the habit of watching the news every evening, yet doing so leaves you distraught and anxious. You can quit watching the news and go to language class instead. Or perhaps you have the habit of going online every day, checking your Facebook page or surfing the Internet with no particular destination in mind after checking e-mail; and yet it consumes 20 to 40 minutes every day (if not more). Exchange the bulk of your time spent online for a creative effort.

It may seem impossible to find the time, and your ego will certainly object, but do it anyway. Resist your ego's objections, and go for the experience with as little negative self-talk as possible. Be aware of the potential sabotage you may encounter, and ready yourself for it. Don't fight it, though; just ignore it. Following your Spirit is worth the initial discomfort. Try it for 40 days and see how you feel. Remember that this is the minimum amount of time it takes to establish a new habit. Notice how prioritizing your Spirit rather than your ego makes you feel.

> *"Let the beauty we love be what we do. There are hundreds of ways to kneel and kiss the ground."*
>
> — RUMI (TRANSLATED BY COLEMAN BARKS)

Secret Death Wish

Eric has always been a great guy. Everyone loves him. If anyone, anywhere, had a problem, he was immediately on hand to help. People admired and respected him throughout the small town where he lived. No one suspected he had a secret. They couldn't. What would they think? It would ruin everything. So for years, he didn't admit it—not even to himself.

Eric married his high-school sweetheart 26 years ago. Now, four beautiful daughters later, he was silently suffering from a deep, immovable depression. He endured what he felt had become a sterile, soul-deadening, sexless marriage for a long time. He didn't blame his wife for the way things had deteriorated between them. If anything, he blamed himself.

On paper, Sara was the best partner a person could have. The house was impeccable, and she took care of their daughters like a CEO overseeing a beloved business. Everything was well managed, and their children were supported in every way. From schoolwork and school clothes, to extracurricular activities and Girl Scouts meetings, Sara handled it all like a champ. Eric was grateful not to have to deal with any of it. He believed he wouldn't know how to and regarded his wife as the maestro of all things domestic. He just couldn't figure out when their relationship had gotten so lost—and truthfully, he wasn't sure if he wanted to find it again.

Eric's job was another source of quiet despair. He had a sign business that he'd inherited from his father. It was profitable, and he appreciated his employees. It wasn't that stressful either. It was just that he really hated it and felt bad for feeling that way. He definitely wouldn't admit how he felt. Many people, especially his family, reminded him all too often how he ought to be grateful to have a reliable income, especially when so many others were out of work. Furthermore, the business enabled him to be a good provider, which he prided himself on.

Between his empty marriage and unfulfilling job, Eric's life became more and more depressing. He often avoided his work and procrastinated on things he had to do at home. Then he'd go in the opposite direction and throw himself into his mounting responsibilities in an attempt to make up for the time he had wasted. No matter how he reasoned it or how hard he tried to deny it, he felt trapped. But he wouldn't let himself think about it too much. It was his duty to carry on. He was, after all, responsible. And yet, the older his daughters became, the more he struggled with why he had to be so responsible.

He left or, more accurately, ran away from his home life every chance he got, engaging in risky, high-adrenaline sports, such as rock climbing, downhill ski racing, and high-speed motorcycle rides on steep country hills. He'd do anything to quell the frustration and anger that was boiling inside him. And as he tried to outrun his dissatisfaction, he wondered how he could feel so wrong in spite of his efforts to do things so "right"—at least according to the rules he was given by his parents, church, and whomever else. They were just implied, and so he complied.

One day Eric had a disastrous accident. While riding his motorcycle with a friend at lightning speed down a dirt road, his front wheel was punctured on an unexpected hole and exploded, throwing him 50 feet into the air. He landed headfirst and onto his shoulder. The blow caused a main artery in his neck to burst.

This is it, he thought, almost relieved, as he lay on the ground bleeding. *I'm going to die.* Soon after, he vaguely remembered being airlifted out of the valley and flown to a nearby hospital. He missed the rest and slipped into unconsciousness.

Eric didn't die, although according to his doctors, he should have. Instead, he was miraculously pieced back together and returned to the life he secretly wished to exit. That's when his greatest pain settled in. He could no longer run from his misery as he had tried to before. He couldn't even walk away from it now. He could only lie in bed and think about his life—or take lots of painkillers to forget about it, but they made him extremely nauseated so that wasn't really an option. He had to face his feelings, and that scared him more than anything.

Eric's body recovered over time, but his inner struggle continued. Having to slow down, even stop, and being forced to think about his present situation all day long was excruciatingly difficult. Then one day he overheard a conversation between two women about the idea of a person's Spirit. It was subtle, yet strong enough to make him notice. He wasn't even sure what the word meant, so he Googled it and learned that it's from the Latin *spiritus,* or "breath," and refers to the noncorporeal body of a human.

The "noncorporeal"—the part that's not my skin and bones. Not even the brain matter in my head, he thought. *Interesting. No one in my life has ever talked about that. . . .*

The minute Eric opened the door to Spirit, something inside him woke up. He instinctively knew what it was. It was the feeling he had been running from all these years. It was his Spirit that had been chasing him, trying to get his attention. And to his surprise, it was his own self that he was afraid of.

His cloud of depression eased a little and was replaced by overwhelming curiosity. Like a detective who has discovered a key to a secret treasure chest, he unlocked his heart and decided to explore. His Spirit was waiting there to meet him. Eric took a deep breath, and for the first time in years, actually made contact. It felt real and genuine, and thankfully, very good.

Why am I so afraid of my Spirit? he wondered for days and weeks afterward. Bit by bit, the answer revealed itself. It was because his Spirit revealed the truth that his life was artificial. The person he carried himself as in the world—the one everyone loved and applauded—wasn't who he really was inside. He was an actor, a fake. He realized that he'd given up his true nature long ago in order to please others.

Eric listened even more deeply to his heart by meditating, practicing yoga, slowing down, and taking recuperative walks. As he did so, he talked with his Spirit and listened intently for clues, for any guidance on how to feel better. In time, his Spirit showed him how most of his actions were done automatically—without thinking (or even wanting to think), and most of all, without any regard for himself. It was almost as if he were playing the part of a superhero with a magic cape that he'd put on the minute there was a call for help. He liked the attention in the beginning because it made him feel special and important. But now he only felt suffocated and trapped by his persona.

Through his Spirit, Eric intuited that he had shut out his wife because he didn't like feeling close to her. It was too scary, too vulnerable, too close for comfort. They were like actors in a play called *Married Life;* and when the play went from that to *Family Life,* he lost the starring role. He found himself in the background, and it wasn't fun or fulfilling—at least not in the way he decided to play his part.

The more he listened to his Spirit, the more scared yet relieved he became. He was afraid because he knew he couldn't continue living a lie, but he also didn't know how to undo what seemed so set in stone. The relief he experienced was because at least now he felt authentic and didn't have to hide his secret, at least not from himself.

Several times he wanted to deny everything and go back to the miserable, unconscious life he had lived before his accident. Yet he knew he couldn't. He was a dead man in that life. The accident was just his way to confirm this truth to others. As hard as it was to look at the mountainous mess he needed to extricate himself from—and face the upset it would cause the people he loved—he knew he had to begin for his Spirit's sake. His world was imploding anyway. At least he felt a genuine heartbeat of excitement for the first time in a long, long while.

Once Eric connected to his Spirit, he couldn't keep his secret from others much longer. One by one, starting with his wife, he told everyone the truth. He explained that he wanted—no, he *needed*—a different life, a different job, and a different kind of personal relationship. He craved a different identity, one that wasn't trapped by feeding off the approval of others.

What happened after his confession surprised him. He expected a catastrophic reaction—sure that his revelation would destroy his wife, shock his friends, hurt his children, ruin his reputation, and embarrass his parents. But none of his fears were realized. Everyone just listened to what he had to say and told him that they had known all along: "We just want you to be happy. Please do what you have to do for all of our sakes!"

And so Eric's second life began. He threw away his Superman cape—mentally, that is. He kept his sign business going but also took up woodworking, which he loved, so his job wasn't defining him anymore. He moved out of his home and into a small studio apartment. It was simple: just a bed, a lamp, and a refrigerator. But it was *his* space, and he loved it. He started experimenting with his look and wearing different clothes. He even grew a ponytail for a while but eventually cut it off because it didn't feel right . . . but it did feel right to try.

Has Eric's Spirit led him back to himself? Not entirely, but it has begun to. He hasn't fully found himself because learning to listen to and trust his Spirit is a new process. It's still unfamiliar for him to look inside for guidance when his entire life he'd been listening "out there." On some days, he backslides, but not too far. He's discovering who he really is and surrendering control to his Spirit. His marriage is in a shambles, but his wife loves him, and they're trying to discover what's real between them. His finances are challenged as well, but no one is homeless or hungry.

The most interesting part of the journey is that on some level, everyone in his life has been affected by his shift back to a more authentic self. They are curiously watching and learning. As upsetting as it has been to the status quo, Eric's decision to follow his heart feels right to all of them. It benefits them, too.

Outwardly, Eric's life is still quite a mess—but it's an exciting, evolving, authentic mess. His children, now young adults, are accepting his changes and asking him a lot of questions. He is finally speaking to them on a genuine, heartfelt level; and they're starting to really get to know each other for the first time. His wife isn't happy that he's living in a studio so that he can find himself, but she isn't totally shattered. She, too, has been positively influenced, even if it wasn't something she sought out or even wanted. She's asking the same questions of Spirit that Eric began asking after his accident. That's how the power of Spirit works: As one person wakes up, he or she awakens another and another and so on. The day will eventually come when all of us will be awake.

Eric and his wife aren't sure about the future of their marriage. They know that they love something inside each other, but they have to find it in themselves first. This is the only way *real love* is possible . . . and that is what the power of Spirit is all about.

Making the Shift

To surrender to the power of Spirit, you must listen to your heart and admit how you feel, first to yourself and then to others, even if your truth makes you or those around you uncomfortable, unhappy, angry, or afraid. Admitting your true feelings will make you vulnerable, so the ego tries to keep you from doing this at all costs. But it's only when you embrace your vulnerability and surrender control that you can connect to the power of your Spirit. It is the only way to heal your life.

Keep in mind that shifting from the power of your ego to the greater power of Spirit necessitates change in many or, perhaps, most of the things in your life. Change can be scary, so once again, your ego will try to distract you and convince you to suppress the truth. This doesn't work, however, as your Spirit can be ignored for a while but not silenced. Your feelings might be temporarily buried, but they will never go away. Instead, they turn into anger, depression, and irritability.

It can be scary to look at your life and admit that it isn't working or doesn't feel authentic. To live in alignment with your Spirit is to live your truth and build your life upon it. Trying to hold an artificial existence together is futile and will leave you feeling drained and miserable. You aren't kidding anyone—your unhappiness is felt by others. Remember that your unlimited creative power is available to you and all those who could benefit from it as soon as you release control and embrace your Divine self.

Asking the Questions

Now take out your journal and turn your attention inward. Contemplate each of the following questions, and invite your Spirit, your most authentic self, to respond to each one. Give yourself plenty of time to feel the genuine response coming from your heart, the source of your power.

- Where in your life is your Spirit expressing the need for change?

- In what ways are you feeling out of touch with your feelings? Why do you think this is so?

- Are you keeping a secret or running away from your Spirit?

- Are you afraid of the changes that your Spirit is now urging you to make?

- Are you fearful of being authentic with the people in your life?

- What do you fear most? What do you internally struggle with?

- What does your ego hold on to? Are they aspects of yourself or your life that no longer feel authentic? How does that make you feel?

- If you were to admit to yourself and the world what your Spirit longs for right now, what would it be? Have you embraced this truth, or are you trying to ignore it?

- How do you feel after answering these
  questions? Check in with your inner self,
  and take your time before answering. Relax
  and listen. Don't rush.

After writing down your answers, set aside your journal and remain seated. Close your eyes, and calmly breathe in and out through your nose. Start with a sigh or two to help you relax. Listen to your Divine self. If you could change something in your life, what would it be? What is your heart telling you?

With your next breath, let all of your tension go and simply *be* for a moment or two, even longer if possible. Enjoy sitting and breathing deeply, empty of all thought, free of any agenda, and in the moment. Feel this vibration of being connected to Source. Notice how peaceful, content, and even energized you feel. This is the power of your Spirit, and it's available to you at all times. It is the real you. *Remember this.*

Daily Practice: Speak from Your Heart

Speak from your heart, even if it frightens you. This may first involve discovering your truth, especially if you've been inauthentic all of your life.

Start by saying the following sentence out loud, every day: "If I weren't afraid, I would . . . " and then complete the statement. Continue speaking out loud, for two to three minutes. If possible, do this in the morning when you're standing at your altar. At least make some time to do this when you won't be interrupted or distracted.

Listen to your responses, and feel the energy they unleash within you. Compare them to your present situation. Where is the disparity? How big is it? Is the life you are presently living somewhat near the life you long for? Are parts of it exactly as you want them to be? What parts aren't? Tune in to the energy in your heart around the parts of your life that you don't want. How would you describe it? Do you feel restless, agitated, hopeless, afraid, hurt, trapped, or dead? Now feel the energy in your heart around the life you envision. How would you describe this energy? Do you feel more relaxed, more peaceful? Are you suddenly more confident and satisfied? Today, take one step in the direction your Spirit longs for.

If you want a different job, begin the process. If you want to work for yourself, write down your ideal job description. If you crave time alone, make the decision to take it and mark it on your calendar. If you want a change, tell the people it would most affect that you're intending to make some shifts in your life. Be calm and don't ask for permission when sharing your truth. Be kind and compassionate, and have respect for others' reactions. Change scares everyone and can bring up the fear of abandonment. Simply explain that you've abandoned yourself and must return to your truth before you can be genuinely present in the best possible way to others. Ask the people in your life for their love and support. Don't expect them to agree with what you're doing—they may not, and that is their right.

Follow your Spirit regardless of the circumstances. Invite others to explore the truth with you, but don't insist. Choosing to connect to the power of Spirit is a personal calling and comes to each of us in the right time. You cannot force this desire on someone else, so don't try to. Listen to others' fears if they react, but don't defend your intention. You have the right and the need to transform, be authentic, and live your highest truth. The Universe requires that of all of us. Following your Spirit liberates and serves everyone in the end, even if it's a disruptive, messy process along the way. Be loving *and* courageous.

Every single day, take one definitive step in the direction of your authentic self. If you're afraid to surrender to your Spirit, admit it, but take that one step anyway. As you do, notice how the All-Loving, All-Powerful Source, the Divine Holy Power of Life meets you halfway. Pay attention to how you feel as you choose to allow your Spirit to lead your life as opposed to being led by your fears.

Throughout the process, note how your body feels, how you sleep, how you breathe, and even how your heart feels. How does the world around you feel? Write this down in your journal. Like undertaking a grand experiment, it's vital to take action every day, even if it's just baby steps, and be aware of the changes these actions bring about. Let your experience be your guide— not your thoughts or fears. Breathe and do. One day at a time. Eventually, you'll see that your mind quiets down and stays calm. When this occurs, you're in the process of great transformation.

"This above all—to thine own self be true."

— WILLIAM SHAKESPEARE

The Raging Battle

On the surface, Barbara had everything under control. She was a successful orthopedic surgeon who had built up a significant clientele over the years. She had been married to a decent man for more than 30 years, and together they raised two responsible sons, who were both currently enrolled in medical schools at highly prestigious colleges. She was extremely proud of her children.

Barbara, with some help from her husband, had paid off their home; amassed a solid retirement account; and in addition to financing her sons' education (which was considerable), she also managed to pay all the bills without too much trouble. She definitely ran a tight ship and felt that she did a good job. Yet, in spite of all these positive accomplishments, she often felt frustrated and unhappy—a fact that she couldn't hide very well.

To make matters worse, she was ashamed of her chronically petulant state of mind and would chastise herself because other people suffered with "real" problems and challenges. This thinking only made her feel even more guilty and angry with herself for not being at peace.

In an attempt to relax, she consulted a psychotherapist, who, after many sessions, suggested that her mental state might be rooted in a chemical imbalance. Therefore, her therapist prescribed an anti-anxiety medication to assist in balancing and calming her moods. Open to trying anything that might help her step out from under the persistent storm cloud, she agreed. But even that failed to make a difference. After six months on the medication, she didn't feel any better—in fact, her agitation grew worse.

From time to time, Barbara tried to justify her sour outlook by finding things around her to blame it on. Yet deep down, she knew those things weren't the issue. Her agitation signified something else: her Spirit was angry, and she could no longer ignore it.

For many years, Barbara's ego had trapped her into living an overly controlled, overly responsible, and overly ambitious life. In the meantime, she ignored her Spirit and placed it under "house arrest" by her militarized routines. She gave little attention or importance to her inner life. Whenever her mental chatter quieted down, her Spirit would try to get her to ease up on her relentless pursuit of external commitments and allow room to experience a gentler, natural, and more rewarding way of life. But she stubbornly refused to listen. Instead, she marched on, keeping it "all under control." The longer she refused to listen to her Spirit, the angrier it became. Her ego and Spirit were at war.

Barbara wasn't in the dark about what was going on within her. She knew she had to stop being the great giver to all, the control freak, and face her own needs and vulnerabilities in order for a change to take place. She knew she had to act on her Spirit's urgings—the ones she couldn't justify or considered silly and a waste of time. Her inner self *needed* to feel supported. She *needed* to relax. She *needed* to do nothing at all once in a while. Most of all, she knew her Spirit needed space to breathe, feel, and meditate. She needed to look out the window of the beautiful home she'd created and hear her own thoughts. She needed to walk in nature and sit among the trees. She needed to stop thinking and doing and just be. She knew she should let others carry their own load, but her ego didn't want to give up control. So it fought long and hard to keep her Spirit from taking over, and her inner battle raged on.

Barbara's ego was afraid. After all, she could count on herself, but to step back and count on others or on life itself was quite another thing. If she listened to her Spirit and released control, then things could possibly fall apart. If that happened, she would have nothing and no one to save her. And that, she resolved, as her fears spiraled out of control, was something she could never allow.

But Barbara's Spirit would no longer be silent. It was fighting for her authentic life. Her Spirit announced itself everywhere. It spoke through her increased impatient outbursts with her staff and even her patients. It spoke when she would go straight to her bedroom once she got home after work, declining all social invitations and asking to be left alone.

Barbara knew this internal battle had to stop, and so did everyone else. Thankfully, her family stepped up to the plate. Due to her increasingly "crazy" behavior, they had an intervention of sorts and insisted that she take time off from her responsibilities and rest. Secretly, she was relieved. She wanted to surrender to her Spirit and give up control, but she was deathly afraid of the consequences. When her family demanded that she stop and take care of herself, it was as if a Divine force had stepped in and given her the permission she needed.

Barbara turned her practice over to a trusted colleague and went on an indefinite sabbatical. It took her nearly three months to regain enough energy before she could even start to tune in to a deeper connection with her Spirit. But she was on her way. Bit by bit, she made progress. Slowly, Barbara surrendered more and more to her Spirit and rediscovered what joy and pleasure felt like. Relief came in small surges, as she allowed Divine support to flow in.

She started to recognize what filled her up and also what drained her. To her surprise, she discovered that much of what had made up her life before her "break" was fulfilling and meaningful. She loved being a doctor and helping others. It just couldn't be a one-way street of willful intent anymore.

No matter how hard she worked to keep things under control, she knew it was time to step back and let her Spirit guide her. She realized that life wasn't something to control. It was something to allow and experience, to learn from and enjoy; and her Spirit was frustrated with her for refusing this gift. Her unhappy, angry state was an honest reflection of her willful self-neglect and rejection of the goodness of life. Now that the internal fire of her Spirit was doused, she understood the futility of pretending that she was, or could be, in charge of everything at all times.

Eventually Barbara returned to work, but she cut down her hours significantly. She and her husband sold their expensive home and bought a townhouse closer to the office. She planted her first garden in their small backyard, putting her hands in the ground for the first time in her life. It cooled her agitation like no medication ever could. In the rich earth, she found a source of energy that gave her something that rejuvenated her soul—and she couldn't get enough. Gardening became her passion, her play, her meditation, and her prayer. She felt in direct contact with Source when she was alone with her plants, so she was finally able to stop trying to *be* the Source as she had done in the past.

Tending to her garden taught her how to surrender. While she was the one who cared for her plants, she couldn't control how much they grew. In admitting this, she learned to respect and trust the Divine forces greater than her own ego. This calmed her intellect and allowed her to quit trying to save the world. It didn't need saving. She was part of it—she didn't need to run it.

Barbara marveled at the intensity with which she had resisted surrendering to her Spirit for so long. It wasn't like she was ever truly confused about what she needed to do to feel whole and peaceful. Intuitively, she knew. In retrospect, she realized that her resistance came from confusing surrender with submission, and she didn't want to lose herself any more than she already had.

On the other side of her transformation, living at peace with her Spirit, she discovered that to surrender means to allow something greater to take over and nourish her—not strangle her as her ego had feared. When she let go, her Spirit led her to a much simpler, more internally spacious life. This is what she secretly desired all along, but couldn't see a way to make possible. It wasn't until she surrendered that the solutions and support showed up. And to her great surprise, nothing collapsed—another illusion of her ego lifted. In fact, her orthopedic practice remained quite stable and not one patient left.

Laughing, she said, "I now recognize how much I overrated my importance to all these people. The truth was that I had it backward. They were my foils because with them I could hide from myself. Stepping away from my own rat race, I finally saw what everyone else could see all along. I'd lost my Spirit, and I was only fooling myself into thinking that I didn't need it."

Making the Shift

The Holy Spirit is the Divine fire in you, the spark of life, the creative catalyst for all things; and it must be expressed. If not, it finds outlets elsewhere, often ones that are undesirable and can even feel destructive. The fire of your Spirit wants to clear away the things that block your authentic self, because they're stealing your life force. Sometimes your inner fire turns to rage when you try to control it or put it out, as it did with Barbara. Or your fire may be redirected in passive-aggressive ways, causing you to lash out at family and friends in order to relieve your internal conflict. If you suppress your inner fire deeply enough, it turns so far inward that it can even disturb your health. It can do any of these things to get your attention.

No matter how it expresses itself, your Spirit will not be denied forever. Eventually, your inner fire will ignite and help you create an authentic life, filled with energy and awe; or it will "burn the house down," liberating you from the very prison cell built up by your ego. You decide.

One way or another, all of us will surrender to the fire of our Spirit, because doing so will allow us to tap into our personal power. The first commandment tells us not to have false gods. This speaks directly to the fear-based illusions of the ego-mind that keep us from connecting to the Divine spark within, making us dependent upon

141

external things or our own misguided attempts to be in control at all times.

When we humble ourselves and let go, our inner Spirit is channeled to creative and magnificent ends, expanding and evolving to unlimited horizons. Unless we surrender, however, we cut ourselves off from our Divine power and burn out. Then we're left to rise from the ashes and find our way back to Source once again. In the end, there is no other place to go.

Asking the Questions

Now take out your journal and turn your attention inward. Contemplate each of the following questions, and invite your Spirit, your most authentic self, to respond to each one. Give yourself plenty of time to feel the genuine response coming from your heart, the source of your power.

- What are you feeling most annoyed, irritated, or angry about?

- In what ways are you feeling burned out? Describe how you feel mentally and physically.

- What is your ego attached to most? Are there certain areas in your life that you can't release control of?

- What are you most insecure about or afraid of? In what areas of your life do you feel that you really need support right now?

- Do you feel the fire of your Spirit within? Are you burning with passion and creativity, or smoldering with frustration?

- Can you sense the energy and spark that Source delivers?

- What must you let go of in order to feel more Divine fire in your life?

- If you were to completely surrender to your Spirit, what would change in your life?

- In what areas of your life do you most feel the need of support for now?

After writing down your answers, set aside your journal and remain seated. Close your eyes, and calmly breathe in and out through your nose. Start with a sigh or two to help you relax. Is your inner fire burning bright? Surrender control so that your Spirit can ignite your passion and creative spark.

With your next breath, let all of your tension go and simply *be* for a moment or two, even longer if possible. Enjoy sitting and breathing deeply, empty of all thought, free of any agenda, and in the moment. Feel this vibration of being connected to Source. Notice how peaceful, content, and even energized you feel. This is the power of your Spirit, and it's available to you at all times. It is the real you. *Remember this.*

Daily Practice: Keep Your Fire Burning

Tend to the fire of your Spirit daily. Every morning, gently stretch, move, bend, or walk for at least ten minutes shortly after awakening. Whether expressed in a few yoga postures, a trip to the gym, or a simple walk around the block, physical movement keeps your Spirit burning strong and channels its power toward your highest creative expression. Being stagnant or spending too much time "in your head" causes the fire to die out.

It's important to keep an eye on your inner fire. Direct its power by sitting in quiet meditation for at least five minutes a day after your morning movement. In yoga, this balance is achieved through savasana, which means taking a few moments to quietly meditate and relax following the more active yoga asanas, or positions. Sit in your own version of savasana, and listen to the Holy Spirit. Surrender your mind to Spirit, and let its fire be the force that moves you.

> *"Walk in the light of your own fire,*
> *and in the flame which ye have kindled."*
>
> — ISAIAH 50:11

The Ultimate Surrender

Bianca had gone through a terrible three-year period. Her beloved father was in a horrific accident at work that left him in a coma and paralyzed from the neck down. He never fully regained consciousness, and after two agonizing years in the hospital, he finally died. The impact of his death was devastating to the family, but especially to Bianca's younger brother, who fell into a deep depression. Feeling so overwhelmed and demoralized, and unable to get over his father's passing, he took his own life, further shocking and crippling Bianca and her mother and sister.

Thankfully, her husband, who was her rock, kept her and their three young children going. Bianca ran a medical clinic for underprivileged women and couldn't afford to collapse into a state of emotional despair, for financial reasons as well as a personal obligation to the community she served.

Bianca had a strong connection to her Spirit and knew in her mind, if only sometimes in her heart, that these horrendous losses might make sense one day. At the very least, she knew that eventually she might be able to accept what had happened and come to some sense of peace. This awareness kept her sane. In the meantime, she had to remain strong for her clients, as well as for her mom and sister, who both seemed ready to collapse and give up. But most important, she had to appear cheerful for her children, who were still quite young and deserved a happy mother. She made sure to grieve out of sight and on the go.

Through early morning walks, late-night talks with her husband, and lots of daily prayer, Bianca managed to stay aloft. She took days off when she could, saw a massage therapist on occasion, went out to lunch with close friends, and practiced gratitude for everything in her life. She knew she had to be proactive and responsible for her own spiritual well-being, and that for some unknown reason, losing her family was a lesson she had to undergo. She had to surrender to life as it unfolded, and she did her very best to do so.

It wasn't easy, as her emotions often clouded the scene. Her mother angered her with her constant negativity, acting so helpless and victimized, as if the loss was hers alone, while ignoring the fact that Bianca was suffering as well. Her sister was a little better. At least they could commiserate together when they needed to vent, both struggling with their mother and her self-absorbed grief, while also trying to console each other. It helped.

All in all, as sloppy and slow as it was, her efforts to surrender were working. She wasn't sure if she was surrendering to her Spirit or simply resigning herself to the circumstances life had dealt her, but she was doing her best. Eventually she had even recovered enough of her inner spark to suggest to her husband that they go to Disneyland for vacation, something the kids had begged them to do for years. In the spirit of getting on with life, it was time. Everyone was overjoyed.

Off they went on a wonderful family adventure, staying at one of the Disney hotels, enjoying the park to its fullest. Even Bianca admitted that it was a great, if occasionally tiring, vacation. The kids were entertained beyond their wildest imaginations, and their joy was infectious. It uplifted her.

After a week of fun and sun, they boarded their plane back home. They were on a smaller-sized aircraft and were seated near the back, all in one row. The flight was uneventful until they were close to landing. They flew into severely stormy weather with intense turbulence. They were on approach to land and experienced sudden wind shears just before touchdown, which nearly flipped over the airplane. The pilot aborted the landing. The lurch in her gut from this sudden drop was beyond anything Bianca had just paid to experience at Disneyland. This was truly frightening. Many passengers on the plane screamed in terror, and then everyone was silent.

The weather was so bad that it looked black outside. The plane was rocking violently when Bianca suddenly realized they were all going to die. At first she grabbed hold of her children's hands, although her son pushed her away. She started to recite the Hail Mary out loud, over and over again, almost as if in a trance, as the rest of the passengers remained silent in abject fear.

A second attempt was made to bring the plane in, and the same thing happened. The wind shears were so severe that the pilot again had to abort the landing at the last minute, and they rocketed through the storm, trying to regain altitude. Bianca couldn't stop praying, all the while thinking, *At least my family is together. When we die, no one will be left behind.*

Then something miraculous occurred. Bianca stopped fighting the experience they were in and completely surrendered to it instead. If they were going to die, she thought, that also meant that they were going to see God. She was suddenly overcome by a sense of profound peace and joy. It was unlike anything she had ever felt. For the first time in her life, she wasn't desperately fighting something or trying to hold on. In a wave of deep relaxation, she completely let go. Hugging her kids, even her son, who had somehow relaxed as well, they sat together serenely. In fact, she noticed that the more peaceful she was, the more her family followed her lead. It even seemed to spread in waves to other passengers. She could tell because many of the people near her were breathing regularly, almost in unison.

The storm outside was raging, but the one in her heart seemed to have lifted. She wondered if her father had felt this way before he died. She even wondered whether her brother had experienced it before he took his life. If so, she understood why he would go through with it. Never before had she felt such peace, knowing that she and her precious family would soon return to God, to Source.

The pilot approached the runway for the third time. This time, the plane slammed down hard on the ground and skidded, but they made it. After a moment of stunned silence, the passengers erupted into a roar of applause. The nightmare was over. They were alive and safe.

Yet Bianca was not the same woman. Somehow during that harrowing experience, she had managed to completely surrender. She let go of trying to make life move one way or another—instead, she fully experienced what was. Her mind stopped trying to control everything, and her heart burst wide open. It didn't matter if she died that day. She'd discovered what lies beyond this realm, beyond her control . . . and it was beautiful beyond belief.

Something else also happened. She realized at the same time that there was no reason to resist the earthly realm either. In other words, life wasn't meant to be controlled, managed, resisted, judged, or feared. It was just meant to be lived, and that was something she had been afraid of. But now she knew there was no right or wrong way—she was just supposed to fully experience everything. Right after the plane miraculously landed, Bianca burst out laughing, overcome with joy. She was so thankful they made it, because she knew she had a lot of living to make up for. Since the Holy Spirit had decided to give her more time, she didn't want to waste another moment feeling bad.

To Bianca, life had never looked or felt so good. Her children were miracles before her eyes. Her husband was beautiful. The blue sky, just peeking through the now lifting heavy clouds was spectacular. Colors seemed brighter, the air was crisp, and the sounds around her were music to her ears. She wasn't sure where she had been all these years, but she was present now! And she was no longer afraid. What a relief. What a gift to have been on that plane. She laughed all the way home, and hasn't stopped since.

Making the Shift

The ultimate surrender is to stop living in the past or future, stop yearning for the approval of others, and stop trying to control the situation. Simply experience it instead. This is a profound transformational shift because the ego doesn't know how to do this, and maybe never will. The highest form of surrender is when you free yourself from your ego's perceptions and experience life from the full vantage point of your Spirit. Because you are only temporarily in a physical form, death to this form is inevitable. The ego game is to pretend that it won't happen, but this takes you away from fully living and enjoying life.

Accepting death is the ultimate surrender and the highest form of transformation to Spirit. We have no choice. But when we accept death to the best of our ability, we are given the most powerful gift of life—the freedom to fully live as our authentic selves.

Asking the Questions

Now take out your journal and turn your attention inward. Contemplate each of the following questions, and invite your Spirit, your most authentic self, to respond to each one. Give yourself plenty of time to feel the genuine response coming from your heart, the source of your power.

- Have you experienced the death of a loved one? If so, how did it make you feel?

- Have you ever faced your own death? If so, how has that affected or changed you?

- How do you presently feel about death and dying? Do you ever think about it? Do you ignore it, fear it, or perhaps accept it?

- What ideas do you hold about life after death?

- What connection, if any, have you ever had to the afterlife? For example, have you ever dreamed of someone who died? Have you ever had an out-of-body or near-death experience? Has someone close to you ever had this kind of experience?

- If you knew you were dying, what would you do differently? Can you start doing this now?

After writing down your answers, set aside your journal and remain seated. Close your eyes, and calmly breathe in and out through your nose. Start with a sigh or two to help you relax. Can you let go of any fears you have about death? Connect to your higher self, the power of your Spirit, and release your desire to control life. Feel the profound serenity of Source.

With your next breath, let all of your tension go and simply *be* for a moment or two, even longer if possible. Enjoy sitting and breathing deeply, empty of all thought, free of any agenda, and in the moment. Feel this vibration of being connected to Source. Notice how peaceful, content, and even energized you feel. This is the power of your Spirit, and it's available to you at all times. It is the real you. *Remember this.*

Daily Practice: Live Your Love

Rarely does someone truly know when the hour of death has arrived. Therefore, rather than focusing on when that will happen, this practice asks you to fully live instead. Today—right now—make a list of all the things you want to do or experience before you leave this life. Create your "bucket list," so to speak.

Put this list in a prominent place, one where you can't miss it, and then do one thing toward fulfilling it every day, without exception. Live as if you no longer have the time to put off your dreams or answer to someone else's demands, rather than your own authentic desires. You really don't have the time!

Ignore all the reasons your ego comes up with to make you put this off or believe that other things are more important. Your ego is lying to you once again. There is no reason why you shouldn't live as you wish, starting right now. To do so is genuine surrender . . . and with it comes the gift of life, as your Spirit wants you to fully live.

> *"When we know love matters more than anything and we know that nothing else really matters, we move into a state of surrender. Surrender does not diminish our power; it enhances it."*

— SARA PADDISON

Congratulations on making it this far! Relax and take a deep cleansing breath. Have you made time to incorporate a daily practice into your life? Has it helped you discover your authentic self and connect with your Spirit? Be sure to note how you're feeling in your journal, and keep track of the changes you're experiencing (in yourself and others).

The last stage of transformation is the most exciting of all. Are you ready to enter the flow?

Chapter Six

STAGE FOUR: FLOWING WITH YOUR SPIRIT

When you enter the flow, your ego steps aside and allows your Spirit to completely take over. You receive uninterrupted guidance, direction, solutions, gifts, and even positive surprises from the Universe every day. You place complete trust in the Universe to take care of you in every circumstance and situation you encounter. You can expect assistance with every problem or challenge that arises, and you will receive it.

When you are in the flow, you move through each day in a state of optimism, gratitude, receptivity, and flexibility—ready and willing at any moment to change plans, move in a different direction, and follow your intuition without hesitation or fear. You feel protected because you know you have Divine helpers, both on this plane and in Spirit, who accompany you every step of the way. You expect the best and miraculously attract it, over and over again. Interestingly, it might not be quite what you envisioned, but it will always be the best of what is possible, which is more often than not a much better version than you could have ever imagined.

You feel fully connected to the web of life and move in guided, synchronistic harmony with all, without questioning how things might work out. You simply trust they will. There is no space between you and life, so you experience no interruption or interference from your controlling intellect. Life falls into beautiful co-operation with you, and you with it, in a harmonious dance. One of my clients described flowing with Spirit as "living a charmed life—one that keeps getting better and better." Another referred to it as the "how good can you stand it" experience of life. A third said that it's "God in the driver's seat with you buckled in for the ride of a lifetime with the best chauffeur there is."

Whatever you call it, *flow* is life experienced with ease, grace, peace, healing, and connection. Divine forces behind the scenes connect all the dots of your life, so you can simply enjoy the experience as it unfolds. The best part is the freedom from stress and worry that it offers. You find yourself feeling genuinely carefree and confident, like a well-loved and cared-for child, surrendered in trust.

Mihaly Csikszentmihalyi, in his book *Flow,* refers to this as the optimal human experience. He affirms that people in flow create an inner state of being that brings them peace and fulfillment that's separate from their external environment. In other words, it's an experience that is completely free of the ego's control or fearful response to the outside world. Flow occurs when you relax, accept, live in the present moment, and move in sync with life—rather than struggle against it. When in flow, you and Spirit are one.

Everyone has experienced episodes of flow from time to time—some for a few minutes, some for hours, and some longer. Yet when you become a truly transformed human—living as a Divine being as opposed to a divided and struggling ego-centered being—flow becomes more of a constant. You may have forgetful moments and slip back into a temporary mental state of worry, resistance, and fear; but once you experience flow, these episodes become shorter and are less frequent. Fear and worry cease to torment you as they once may have. Your higher self, your Spirit, leads your life, while your ego-mind, the faithful servant of the Spirit, steps aside. Once you've experienced this, you can trust that you will find it again.

Flow is often perceived as luck by the spiritually unconscious, but there's really nothing lucky or coincidental about it. Flow is faith in action: the synthesis of your true Divine nature merging with your faith in God, the Universe, and life. It is the natural consequence of living as a Divine spiritual being, expressing your most authentic self, and following your intuition. When in flow, you're learning to be a Divine creator, making life an exhilarating and joyous adventure.

Not only is flow a personally beautiful and expanded experience; but your positive energy has an undisputable, immediately infectious effect on others as well. The minute you're around someone who is in flow, your own vibration quickly elevates, and you start to resonate in greater harmony with life. You feel positive, confident, and creative. Your heart opens, and your compassion expands to higher and more perceptive levels.

In other words, you feel inspired, which means *taking the Spirit in.* When your Spirit is "home," fully present in you—moving through your limbs, expressing itself through your mind, living though your heart—everyone around you feels this energy and is profoundly affected.

The Surprise Visit

I was recently reminded of the power of Spirit in flow in the most unexpected way. My family and several of our neighbors decided to have a big barbecue together. We seized upon the idea with great enthusiasm, and it wasn't long before it had extended beyond the neighborhood to include other family members as well.

When our closest neighbors Craig and Sara showed up, they brought along Sara's brother, his wife, and their three kids, including a gawky, painfully shy 14-year-old boy. He sat quietly on the couch and kept to himself the entire time, barely saying a word to anyone. More than once I noticed him sitting alone and asked if he was having fun, and he responded with a faint smile and an unconvincing yes. Obviously preferring that I leave him alone rather than make a lame effort at conversation, I smiled back and left him by himself.

Hours later, the party got livelier, but this young man's demeanor remained the same. He wasn't down—he was just extremely flat, as if no one was home. However, that changed after everyone was finished eating. His mother suddenly announced to all of us that it was time to gather around the piano and listen to her son's latest musical creation. As we walked toward the piano, the boy's dad turned to me and explained that his son had taken only one lesson, so I thoroughly expected this already very shy teen to suffer even more as he was made to perform. Was I ever wrong!

The minute that quiet young man placed his hands on the piano keys, he transformed. He came *alive*. From out of nowhere, his energy shifted, and I could feel his Spirit step in. His fingers flew like lightning across the keyboard, and he unfurled a musical masterpiece that took everyone's breath away. His playing was stunning. Watching him was dizzying; his music was so moving, so heartfelt, that it was as if he'd pulled it right out of heaven. This performance was clearly not streaming from his intellect. After all, he'd taken only one lesson his entire life! No, without question, it was his Spirit playing the piano; and it was so powerful that it humbled us all.

When he finished, everyone—kids and adults—fell silent for a moment and then burst into enormous applause. The power of his Spirit was shining brilliantly through his music, and it flowed with a force of its own. When it was over, people just shook their heads in amazement. There were no words to express the experience.

The most impressive thing about this spontaneous spirited visitation, at least for me, was that it didn't end that night. I still felt its power the next day and clear into the evening. Several times I found myself sharing the experience of him playing with people I ran into. It was too potent to keep it to myself. Later that following night, I wasn't surprised when my friend Debra, who had also been at the barbecue, brought it up while we were chatting. She was still feeling the effects of his spirited concert, too. We laughingly shook our heads in awe, remarking about the tangible power he'd expressed. A moment later, in came my daughter, and without knowing what we were talking about, she also brought up the young piano player's performance and how much it was on her mind. In the end, we all agreed that we'd witnessed something special that made us want to express our own Spirit as authentically and gracefully as he had.

This was a beautiful example of the power of Spirit to uplift, inspire, excite, and activate the vibration and creativity in all people. This boy's Spirit in flow made our Spirits want to flow with his. That is how the power of Spirit works. We may all express our Divine sparks differently, but it is the same Holy Spirit coming through. For the young boy, it was expressed though the piano's keys. For someone else, it might be expressed through the keys of a computer. It may come through baking a pie, planting a garden, or even sweeping the porch. It doesn't matter what we're doing really—what does matter is that when the Spirit is doing the "doing" of our life, it becomes magical.

We all have things we must tend to every day. If our ego is solely in charge, we might undertake them in a begrudging, long-suffering, resentful, or unloving way. The work gets done, but the effort drains us and those around us. But if we allow our Spirit to express through us and let it be the "doer," whether in work or play, the act itself instantly becomes a powerful expression. It is "love made visible," as the famous Lebanese-American novelist and poet Kahlil Gibran wrote in his beautiful book *The Prophet*.

If each of us would flow with the natural expression of our Spirit in all that we do, we would serve to awaken it in others, and soon the entire planet would gracefully flow together. I believe that this is the Divine plan. We just have to get on with it! That is what the grand transformation from ego to Spirit is all about.

Making the Shift

Entering the flow of your Spirit isn't as challenging or far-out as it may seem—despite what your ego may be telling you. You've already experienced flowing with your Spirit in one way or another, as evidenced by the times you've become so engaged and immersed in doing something you love that you lost all track of time and space. You were so content, so happily involved in the experience, that you felt as if you could carry on forever.

When in flow, we are love in motion. Time, space, and separation from life cease to exist. We merge with our experiences and become one. Whether it's cooking a meal, doing the laundry, or washing the car, all of us have flowed with things that we've loved to do and express at one point or another—probably more often than we realize. We just need to learn to be in the flow a lot more.

Asking the Questions

Now take out your journal and turn your attention inward. Contemplate each of the following questions, and invite your Spirit, your most authentic self, to respond to each one. Give yourself plenty of time to feel the genuine response coming from your heart, the source of your power.

- What do you love doing? Do you love to sing, dance, or play an instrument? Do you love going to work every day or playing with your kids? Do you love to golf, exercise, do yard work, or go jogging with your dog? Be specific. How do you feel when you're doing what you love?

- What can you do so well that it's a pure joy to do it?

- When you're deeply engaged, can you sense that your Spirit is taking over? How would you describe flowing with your Spirit to someone?

- Recall a moment when you were so fully engaged in something that you lost all track of time. What were you doing?

- If you could do anything you wanted to, what would you do? This doesn't have to be work related—it can be anything at all.

- When was the last time you experienced someone else in flow? What was he or she doing? How did it affect you?

- When was the last time you felt clearly out of flow? What were you doing? What were you resisting at the time?

- Where do you feel most in flow in your life? Where do you feel least in flow?

After writing down your answers, set aside your journal and remain seated. Close your eyes, and calmly breathe in and out through your nose. Start with a sigh or two to help you relax. Think about something you love to do, and tune in to the way your body feels. When you're aligned with your genuine Divine self, you're flowing with your Spirit.

With your next breath, let all of your tension go and simply *be* for a moment or two, even longer if possible. Enjoy sitting and breathing deeply, empty of all thought, free of any agenda, and in the moment. Feel this vibration of being connected to Source. Notice how peaceful, content, and even energized you feel. This is the power of your Spirit, and it's available to you at all times. It is the real you. *Remember this.*

Daily Practice: Go with the Flow

Going with the flow means accepting life exactly as it is. If you're stuck in traffic, for example, flow with the slower pace rather than honking your horn and cursing at the "idiots" on the road. If you're in a hurry at the grocery store and the checkout line is at a standstill, take a few breaths, smile, and laugh at the tabloid headlines rather than complaining or crowding the people ahead of you to get things moving. If you're working on a project and run into every possible obstacle, step back, take a short break, and adjust your approach to allow some space to enter and relieve the logjam.

In other words, make it a habit to *relax*. Let go. Take a breath and look around. Enjoy the view. Accept life as it unfolds, rather than try to force it in a particular way. Don't complain just for the sake of it, or struggle as a matter of habit. Don't fight to be first. Be patient, and turn to the Holy Spirit for guidance instead. Be aware, listen, and move in accordance with its vibration. Meet what comes your way with grace. Flowing with your Spirit is when you acknowledge the beauty, wisdom, and purpose of what is and cooperate with life as opposed to fighting against it.

You may experience setbacks, but everyone does at times. It's not uncommon to lose your patience (or your temper) and feel tempted to give someone a piece of your mind or want to tell someone else how he or she "should" be living. But reactions and patterned responses like these simply take you out of the flow. They're also upsetting to you and others. Resistance accomplishes nothing of value. Even if you manage to force someone into doing things your way, the negative energy that goes along with your "win" isn't worth the fight. You will experience the backlash of such bullying later on—count on it. You'll get much further in life by feeling and following the flow than you will by bumping up against it.

This doesn't mean that you should be passive or meek. You just need to be aware of the energy around you and use it instead of letting it drain you and others. Take, for example, those who practice martial arts. They follow the flow and use the energy coming toward them to diffuse an attack rather than resist it. The force of the attacker is absorbed and transformed. The end result is that the martial artist remains safe, protected, and above all, peaceful, grounded, and unafraid.

When you do have a setback, catch yourself and make adjustments as quickly as possible. Use your breath to reenter the flow. Remember to always relax, accept, allow, enjoy, and flow.

*"Flow with whatever is happening and let
your mind be free. Stay centered by accepting
whatever you are doing. This is the ultimate."*

— ZHUANGZI

The Ebb

The greatest challenge to staying in flow comes when
you encounter "the ebb," which is any change, expected
or unexpected, that leaves you feeling threatened and
insecure because you aren't sure what's coming next.
You may wonder or worry if you can handle it, if the
change will be harmful or difficult, or even if you will
be safe.

Ebbs occur all the time. They are natural because
all things eventually change—nothing remains the
same indefinitely. Life moves in cycles, and when you
encounter an ebb, it just means that it's time for that
cycle to change. Ebbs occur on a global scale as well as
in a more personal aspect. A global ebb may come about
as a dramatic shift in the current state of the economy or
government; or it might appear as an extreme climate or
environmental change, such as an earthquake, volcanic
eruption, hurricane, or tsunami, among other things.
These natural ebbs have been around since the beginning of time and will continue till the end of time.

Ebbs arise as our personal life cycles shift. We enter
an ebb, for example, when we go from being at home
all day to our first day of school, which means leaving
the familiarity and safety of our caregivers and entering the unknown. For some children, this feels like a
catastrophe, but in the end, these same kids learn to

adjust, grow, and eventually come to greatly enjoy this new experience. We usually kick and scream when the ebbs of life arrive, but if we choose to respond to them as creative conscious Spirits, these changes activate great evolutionary leaps, liberating us from unnecessary and illusory dependencies that we no longer need.

So ebbs don't necessarily feel good, but they are important disruptions because they instigate growth that we wouldn't ordinarily do on our own. We are invited to reflect on where we are, become aware of patterns that hold us back, and enter a new cycle that pushes us ahead. Ebbs require us to let go of ego complacencies and engage our authentic selves so that we can be fluid, flexible, creative, and solution-oriented. We detach from the false gods or outer circumstances of the world for our sense of safety and protection. It's a time to remember that while we are in human form having a creative experience in the world, we are spiritual beings not of this world. The climactic ebb in the human experience is transitioning into death, leading to the flow of rebirth in our Spirit form.

As conscious beings entering the great transformation from *Homo sapiens* to *Homo spiritus,* we must expect, even embrace, the ebb and be willing to move in an often unexplored or different direction without hesitation. This can feel extremely destabilizing and threatening to the ego (which is the Divine plan), causing us to feel anxious, stressed, victimized, overwhelmed, and powerless. That's why it is important to expect periods of ebb in the flow of life, and recognize that this is a signal from our Spirit to grow.

Even though ebbs are unwelcome to the ego, which wants to be in control and doesn't like change, they remind us that the ego never really was in control. The ebbs of life invite us to flow no matter what, and especially to flow in a way that is compatible with change. Ebbs activate the Spirit to override the ego and creatively respond to life by reaching inside and freeing up new insights and solutions. The ebbs of life can be viewed as psychic calisthenics for the Spirit, which take away our mental crutches and make us stronger, freer, and more powerful.

Entering a cycle of change can feel dramatic, scary, and threatening—as if your very self is under attack—but if you remember to surrender to your Spirit and go with the flow, the ebb will guide you to better and better versions of yourself. When the ebb appears in the flow, it simply means that a greater version of you is ready to make its appearance.

I experienced an intense and unexpected ebb many years ago when the job I held at the time, as an international flight attendant, suddenly came to an end. The union I belonged to declared a strike, and we all walked out. Being young and unhappy with certain aspects of my job, I eagerly joined my co-workers on the picket line but fully expected to return to work after a few days of company-versus-union arguments. I figured I'd quickly be back to flying to Paris and London in no time at all.

Instead, all of the striking flight attendants were immediately replaced with new hires, and the door to our jobs closed behind us with a slam. I was so shocked, so insulted, that I just couldn't believe it. That wasn't at all what I had expected to occur. "How could the company do this?!" I shouted to my friends and anyone else who would listen. "I was a great flight attendant. I didn't deserve this! The company was evil to do this to all these good people—especially me," I proclaimed with righteous indignation. "Now what will I do to survive?"

But my indignant, furious, insulted, wounded, and most of all, frightened outpouring of feelings didn't change a thing. That didn't stop me from railing against the reality that my circumstances had indeed changed. I didn't want my circumstances to change. I didn't want to be out of a job; I wanted everything to be as it was. The way I knew it to be. My mind was racing: *What about my free airline passes? How will I pay my rent or buy groceries? What about my co-workers who live elsewhere? How will we be able to see each other again? How will I ever get back to Denver to visit my parents? Or go on adventures?* Such big and little unknowns frightened me and left me feeling overpowered by a force far greater than I was.

For weeks, I panicked and fretted. Then I realized, to my surprise, that once I was away from the job, I was actually glad to be free of it. I admitted to myself that I'd never loved it, and truthfully, I'd always felt a bit like an imposter wearing the uniform. I loved the benefits—traveling to new places, meeting new people—but I wasn't using my gifts the way I had wanted to, and that had always bothered me. While I was on strike, I was suddenly free to pursue what I loved and so, void of interference, I turned my full and undivided attention to my spiritual work for the first time in my life.

I began to book readings with clients on a regular basis, many of whom were my flight-attendant friends, and helped them discover ways to work through the job crisis. I also started teaching monthly workshops in my studio apartment. It was the most challenging, exciting, and fulfilling thing I had ever done in my life. I didn't want to stop! I was even able to sign up for dance and yoga classes on a regular basis (another love), which was not possible when I worked as a flight attendant because my schedule had been much too irregular. I never would have done any of this if the strike hadn't occurred. Although I didn't really love my job, I liked it well enough, so I never considered quitting. Thankfully, it quit me.

My worst nightmare surprisingly became my greatest gift. While kicking and screaming though the ebb, I learned to trust my vibes, follow my heart, and begin my true life's purpose and vocation of spiritual and intuitive guidance work, which I still do to this day. Had that ebb not occurred, I might still be a flight attendant and would have missed the joy and satisfaction of living my dream for all these years. And that is a scary thought.

Until the day I lost my job, I had never, ever considered using my talents and working with them full-time. I loved my psychic work, and used it quite a bit, but I never considered it to be the vehicle in which to fully invest my life. Once the ebb subsided, I found myself in a brand-new and far more meaningful and fulfilling flow in life than I would have ever initiated on my own.

In retrospect, I can see clearly just how ready for change my Spirit genuinely was. Behind the fear rose the challenge to push past my limiting circumstances, be creative, and trust my intuition to guide me to the next step, which is exactly what I did.

Although my response to the ebb was sloppy and emotional at first—and my ego milked the drama for all it could—several years later, when I was offered the chance to return to the airline, I couldn't fathom going back. I was way too happy where I was. I still am! Thank goodness for the ebb, because it was necessary for me to get into a higher flow. That is what the ebb in life is all about.

Making the Shift

The ebb of life reveals which attachments no longer serve our soul purpose in the best way, and what keeps us from being of highest service to the planet. It is actually a signal that we're graduating to a certain level of awareness and are now ready to move to the next level. Therefore, we can always expect an ebb to be part of the flow as long as we are in human form, because growth into Divine consciousness is the only purpose for being here.

To be in the flow means to trust that the Spirit within can create a positive outcome out of any circumstance that comes its way, no matter what. To flow is to believe that the Universe is always conspiring for our success as spiritual beings, inviting us to move closer to our more authentic selves.

Asking the Questions

Now take out your journal and turn your attention inward. Contemplate each of the following questions, and invite your Spirit, your most authentic self, to respond to each one. Give yourself plenty of time to feel the genuine response coming from your heart, the source of your power.

- What phase are you in now: ebb or flow?

- What aspect of your life is in ebb? How do you know?

- If you are in an ebb, what does your Spirit want to unleash?

- What unexpected challenges are inviting you to grow?

- Are you clinging to old beliefs or aspects of yourself? In what ways? How does holding on, rather than letting go and growing, make you feel? Are you forgetting that you are a Divine being and instead feeling more like a victim?

- If you are in the flow, when was the last time you were in an ebb? What gifts and talents have the ebb of life revealed that you weren't aware of beforehand?

After writing down your answers, set aside your journal and remain seated. Close your eyes, and calmly breathe in and out through your nose. Start with a sigh or two to help you relax. Think about cycles of ebb during your life. Knowing the end results, can you see the ways in which these personal shifts brought you in deeper alignment with your Spirit?

With your next breath, let all of your tension go and simply *be* for a moment or two, even longer if possible. Enjoy sitting and breathing deeply, empty of all thought, free of any agenda, and in the moment. Feel this vibration of being connected to Source. Notice how peaceful, content, and even energized you feel. This is the power of your Spirit, and it's available to you at all times. It is the real you. *Remember this.*

Daily Practice: Embrace the Ebb

Notice how life flows in cycles. Are you in the flow or in the ebb? If you're flowing with your Spirit, carry on; and if you're in an ebb, accept it. Don't fight against change. Just be aware and acknowledge that all things are in Divine order at all times.

Remember that no one can go through life without encountering ebbs, but you will eventually return to flow. The more consciously you accept this, the more quickly the ebb turns back to flow and the longer the period of uninterrupted flow will continue. When in ebb, recognize that it has great value. Study what the ebb is asking you to release, and move on. It's a signal that it's time to grow—on a soul level, you're ready to advance. Whether in ebb or flow, communicate your true values and priorities, state your goals, and allow your Spirit to lead you.

> *"The lowest ebb is the turn of the tide."*
>
> — HENRY WADSWORTH LONGFELLOW

The Miracle

Emily, a freelance writer, consciously practiced living in flow. On the days that all went according to plan, it was easy. She felt confident and relaxed, even a bit smug that she was "in the know" about higher living.

On the days that life surprised her, however, she felt challenged, annoyed, and afraid. But she was prepared. She knew to breathe, accept, allow, and trust that what was unfolding was in accordance with the Divine plan and not her own. On those days, in spite of her impulse to resist, she surrendered her ego to the reality at hand and accepted life as it was.

It wasn't as simple as it sounded, though. When life was heading into uncharted territory, Emily felt the same way she did when she was first learning to drive: hesitant and self-conscious. Nothing came automatically. She had to stop and think about her responses in order to be certain she was choosing the right ones. Only then would she act. The hesitation created enormous tension in her body, followed by relief when she felt she'd made the correct choice. She got through each day, but her rhythm felt disjointed and stiff. It didn't feel natural to be so consciously deliberate, at least not yet.

But still she progressed, her Spirit-driven responses slowly coming more naturally as her commitment to Divine living improved. Perhaps as a way to reassure herself that going with the flow was the best way to live, she often enthusiastically shared this philosophy with her friends and loved ones. She was so persuasive and dynamic that people even began to seek her out when they felt insecure and threatened. Her "go with the flow" speech calmed them. She spoke with such conviction that they trusted her and allowed themselves to surrender their fears and give it a try.

This all went well when going with the flow meant surrendering control over relatively small issues; or for example, when someone she expected to call didn't call, or when she disagreed with someone and chose to concede rather than argue the point. In the moment, these seemed like important matters, surely affronts to her well-developed ego, but in reality they were trivial and ultimately meaningless battles with no redeeming value. Emily could feel the benefit of letting go of her knee-jerk responses. What caught her attention, however, was just how much energy she had invested in being "right," judgmental, superior, and critical both of herself and others over the years. It robbed her of the ability to live in the moment in a peaceful, secure way. It was a full-time habit she was in the process of breaking. She was committed to succeeding, but humbled by the enormity of her task.

Emily was making adequate progress and even enjoying a degree of calm when she met with a series of unexpected financial disruptions that put her into a truly vulnerable, even potentially disastrous, position.

First, her two primary magazines changed editors within a matter of weeks of each other, and both cancelled her monthly columns without notice. Her main sources of income vanished overnight, leaving her without enough money to cover the significant rent for her San Francisco apartment. Shortly after that, the IRS sent her a letter stating that she'd misfiled her taxes and owed $47,000, which was due within a few weeks of receiving the notice. She was horrified. Over the years, she'd been living paycheck to paycheck and had virtually no savings. Furthermore, she was a single woman in her 60s and had no kids, family, or friends from whom she would feel comfortable enough to ask to borrow such a large sum of money. She simply didn't have it and had absolutely no way to get it. So she was, in her words, "completely screwed."

For Emily, it was one thing to go with the flow when it came to getting along with others, delivering articles on time, and generally making ends meet by controlling her shopping and other unnecessary indulgences . . . but it was quite another when she was suddenly faced with unemployment, bankruptcy, possible eviction, and a tax conviction by the IRS. All of a sudden "going with the flow" seemed naïve and ridiculous, an irresponsible Pollyanna perspective that ignored the demands of real life.

And yet, what else could she do? Constantly worry? That would hardly solve her problem. Panic? She was already doing that, and it in no way relieved her of her dire straits. Collapse? Even if she did, no one would be there to pick her up and carry her forward. Run away? There was nowhere to go. Besides, even running would cost money, which she didn't have. None of these ego-motivated, victim-based responses provided any more relief than her "go with the flow" approach offered. This was beyond ebb. This was more than a dip in the climb. This was a complete collapse of her system, and she needed rescue in the form of a solution—and she needed it fast.

Her only option was to accept all that she had preached over the years and turn the entire problem over to the Universe and trust that it would help her solve it. In doing so, she first had to face her deepest fears and insecurities, the ones she thought she had long dispelled.

"Why would the Universe help you? After all, you created the problem!" her ego hissed. "If you had been more responsible over the years, this never would have happened. You should have saved. You should have checked on your accountant. You foolishly spent too much money. In fact, given your arrogant and irresponsible behavior, you deserve to go to jail. Shame on you!"

Yes, shame. That is exactly the way Emily felt: completely and utterly ashamed. It was such a deep and old energy that she felt as if she had carried it forever. In fact, she was now sure she was born with it. Feeling it envelop her, she realized it was this exact energy she had been running from her entire life. She thought she had outwitted it with her spiritual practice, only to find herself suddenly trapped. Her shame quickly closed in on her, laughing as if to say, "So you thought you escaped me, did you? You can never escape!"

Emily felt it shroud her entire being, like a dark, life-sucking cloud of death. And yet, she didn't die. She was absolutely miserable, but she wasn't dead. Confronting her deepest, most negative beliefs about herself, in the face of her greatest external fear of being completely out of control and vulnerable, Emily did something she had never done before. She started to laugh. At first, it was a nervous reflex. But soon enough it turned into genuine heartfelt laughter. It was the laughter of a profound realization. She *was* out of control. She hadn't a clue as to how to solve her dilemma. And it didn't kill her. She could relax and quit running. The more she laughed, the better she felt.

She suddenly understood that the only solution was to turn to the Divine to solve the problem and guide her out of it. She realized her spiritual training period was over. She was no longer in the driver's seat when it came to going with the flow of the Universe. She had to graduate, give up her reservations, and completely flow with Divine direction. There was no other way.

It was a leap of faith, and she took it. For the first time, she placed her full confidence and entire well-being in the hands of God and in her higher self. She got down on her knees and prayed for a solution. She didn't lament the problem, as she felt it would be useless to do so. If the Universe was to help, surely it understood the problem better than she did, so there was no need to go over it, further upsetting herself. No, she would not indulge.

Emily prayed for guidance. But as she did, she recognized, perhaps for the first time in her spiritual transformation, a deeper meaning of going with the flow. She wasn't simply to go with just any flow. She needed to align her personal creative intention with the highest flow of Divine creative intention and flow with that. She couldn't just pray to be rescued, as that would reduce her to a passive victim. She needed to pray for inspiration on how to solve the problem herself, to the best of her ability as a Divine being.

She asked to be shown the best way to turn her present situation into a creative example of Divine flow. She prayed with her entire heart and soul to be relieved of all blockages, low self-esteem, and shame (known or unconscious), and to align only with the most creative expression of Divine good she could be in service to. She prayed that her fears would be alleviated so that she could move forward in confidence. She prayed to be free of any disruption of peace in her life. She prayed until she could find no more words to pray. She prayed until her heart was calm and quiet. And then she stopped. As far as anything else she could do, it was done.

At that point, all Emily could do was be patient and wait. She was moved to go back to the work of her daily tasks because she needed to do *something*. So she cleaned her apartment, finished working on a few articles that were due, and walked her dog. And when night came, she went to sleep. Small as they were, those actions felt comforting and right.

She continued her routine for the next couple days, praying all the while to keep her stress at bay. On the third night, she awoke with a start. As soon as she opened her eyes, the idea and title for a book resounded in her mind. And it was a terrific title and a subject she could confidently write about. The minute she stated the title out loud, a wave of relief instantly swept over her. This was it. This was the solution. She immediately wrote it down and lay there in astonishment. She had never, ever considered writing a book, let alone one so clever. As she sat in awe, more ideas on the subject poured into her mind like a rushing river. She found a notebook and started jotting them down, grabbing on to them before they disappeared into the night.

The next morning she called her agent and ran the book idea past her. Not sure how her agent would respond, Emily was greatly surprised and relieved to get just as much enthusiasm from her agent as she herself had felt when the idea first came to her. Her agent suggested that she put pen to paper right away, and she would start attempting to sell the idea.

So Emily wrote, as her agent shopped the title to various publishers. Four weeks later, Emily had her first-ever book contract, along with an impressive advance of $125,000. After paying her agent, she would have enough left over to pay all back taxes, her credit-card debt, and rent for a few months. It was nothing short of a miracle.

But more than the miracle of solving her financial problems of the moment, she experienced the miracle of fully trusting in the Universe to show her how to live as a Divine being rather than a victim. With this new experience as her foundation, she would never again fall back under the illusion that she must live with fear and shame as her truth. She was free and in the creative flow. That's what being a transformed, Divine being means: to live as a full creative partner with the Universe, setting an intention and then being open to the inspiration and guidance for that intention to be realized.

Making the Shift

Going with the flow of the Universe doesn't mean passively surrendering personal creativity and responsibility for the way your life unfolds. Rather, it means living with dynamic creative intention—aligning your personal creativity with the Divine plan so that the fulfillment of your intentions, needs, and desires is Divinely supported, guided, and directed.

Simply put, tell the Universe what you want, but don't tell the Universe how you want it delivered. Leave yourself open to receiving inspiration and intuitive guidance on how best to create your intended desires at all times. Wait in confidence until the flow directs you. It will arrive in the form of intuition. Then follow the intuitive guidance you receive without hesitation or question. That is what it means to go with the flow at the highest level.

Asking the Questions

Now take out your journal and turn your attention inward. Contemplate each of the following questions, and invite your Spirit, your most authentic self, to respond to each one. Give yourself plenty of time to feel the genuine response coming from your heart, the source of your power.

- Have you ever trusted in the Universe for inspiration or direction?

- Are you a student or a seasoned pro when it comes to going with the flow?

- Do you clearly tune in to your intuition? How so? Do you receive intuition through your gut feelings or dreams, or perhaps an overall sense of knowing?

- Do you trust your intuition? In what areas do you trust it the most? When are you hesitant to trust it?

- Are you in the habit of setting intentions and goals? Do you make commitments with confidence, or do you tend to avoid them?

- In what area of your life do you most want to receive guidance and direction right now?

- What are your heart's most important creative desires?

- Do you pray?

- Can you laugh at your fears?

- How has your intuition helped you lately?

- How have you already been inspired and guided by the Universe?

After writing down your answers, set aside your journal and remain seated. Close your eyes, and calmly breathe in and out through your nose. Start with a sigh or two to help you relax. Tune in to your higher self and wait for guidance. Trust your intuition, always remembering that you are a Divine co-creator.

With your next breath, let all of your tension go and simply *be* for a moment or two, even longer if possible. Enjoy sitting and breathing deeply, empty of all thought, free of any agenda, and in the moment. Feel this vibration of being connected to Source. Notice how peaceful, content, and even energized you feel. This is the power of your Spirit, and it's available to you at all times. It is the real you. *Remember this.*

Daily Practice: Set Your Course

Take a few moments each morning to set your intentions for the day. Ask yourself what you would like to accomplish. What is important to your Spirit? In what areas are you in need of inspiration? In what ways would you like to receive support, ideas, and solutions? If possible, announce your intentions and requests out loud, ideally in prayer form.

Your own voice is one of the most powerful sounds in the Universe. As you say your intentions out loud in prayer, you can tell by the vibration behind them whether or not you are genuinely committed to creating these intentions. If you speak with conviction, your Spirit gets behind your intentions and seeks to assist you.

If you speak with hesitation, however, the power of your Spirit refrains from helping you. This is because the Universe co-creates, following your creative lead. The Universe can and will meet you halfway. It will assist the process as long as you ask for guidance and inspiration with pure intention, not as a victim but as a responsible co-creator.

As part of your practice of daily morning prayers, set your intentions and ask for assistance in every way possible. Then open your heart and mind to receive what you ask for in the form of intuition and inspiration. Follow this guidance without hesitation. This is flow in the highest order. Trust your intuitive vibes, and act on them!

*"All you have to do is know where you're going.
The answers will come to you of their own accord."*

— EARL NIGHTINGALE

Coming Full Circle

Sonia, my daughter (she shares my name, as do I with my own mother in a long line of Sonias), and her best friend, Mary, were in the final weeks of college before graduating. They were under a great deal of pressure. Not only were final exams looming before them, and their senior theses yet to be written; but also the extended, emotional good-byes with their dearest friends were adding to their mental and physical overload. Furthermore, they were facing the question of what to do with their lives, which lurked conspicuously at the edges of their minds, burdening their already anxious state.

The job market was the worst it had been in more than 50 years, and the support they enjoyed from their parents as students was soon coming to an end as they stepped into the world. It seemed as if their carefree futures had suddenly contracted into a claustrophobic state of "not enough," and it was terrifying. There wasn't enough time to study, not enough time to say good-bye to friends, not enough inspiration and original ideas to finish their final papers, and not enough money or jobs to support them after their diplomas were placed in their hands. For Sonia and Mary, life seemed overwhelmingly difficult, leaving them both feeling paralyzed.

During one particularly stressful evening, the girls, in a spontaneously rebellious mood, decided to put aside their obligations and go out for drinks and a burger at one of their favorite outdoor cafés in Portland, where they lived. It wasn't really a sensible decision. Not only did they not have the time to indulge in an evening off from their work, but they also didn't have the money to go out and splurge. Rationalizing it all the way to the restaurant as a necessary time-out, they knew that such a choice would catch up with them tomorrow. Still, they were willing to deal with the consequences. My daughter later told me that it was something that they both just felt they needed to do, so they went with it.

No sooner had they sat down and ordered their drinks and meal when they noticed a scary-looking homeless man aimlessly wandering down the street. He was ranting and raving, causing most people to either look away uncomfortably or gaze directly at him in total disgust. He wasn't an unusual sight in Portland since there are a lot of lost people living on the streets there— many of them addicted to alcohol or drugs. Yet as the disheveled man continued weaving back and forth, raging on, he seemed more menacing than most.

Sure enough, he caught Sonia's eye and beelined toward her. Mary groaned as he approached, mostly in fear, as he was clearly unstable and seemed eager to start a fight with anyone who would give him the slightest provocation. Sonia just took a breath and smiled at him.

"I'm hungry!" he screamed indignantly, as he walked right up to their table. "I am a Vietnam veteran, and I fought for this country. Now I'm starving, and no one will even look me in the eye. I just want some food."

Sonia immediately felt compassion for him and calmly said, "I understand. That must be terrible. Please just calm down, and have a seat. I'll order you anything you want to eat."

Still uncertain of his mental state, she pointed toward a table a few feet away from theirs and said, "You can sit there and look this over," as she handed him a menu. "I'll get the waiter."

Surprised by her response, he hesitated and then stormed over to the table she had suggested and threw himself into a chair. He glanced at the menu and then flung it aside just as fast, obviously too distressed or unstable to even read it. Still seething, he defiantly looked right at her and commanded, "I want a cheeseburger, fries, and a chocolate milkshake." He stared angrily toward her as he made the request, as if daring her to refuse.

"No problem," Sonia responded. "I can get that for you. You just sit here. It will come, but it's going to take a few minutes."

By now the waiter recognized that Sonia was trying to help the man, and he joined in the goodwill. He jotted down the order as Sonia dictated, and brought the wretched man a place setting and glass of water. The homeless man refused to look the waiter in the eye. Sonia wondered if that was because he didn't want to risk seeing another look of disapproval coming toward him. She realized that she would probably look away, too, if she were in his place.

Once the waiter left, Sonia encouraged the man to relax, which he seemed to do for about 30 seconds. Then he was up again, pacing back and forth. Suddenly, he stopped in his tracks and looked as if he were seeing a ghost. Sonia, who had been watching him, followed his gaze. Walking down the street toward them was a well-dressed man carrying a briefcase. The homeless man walked right up to him and grabbed his arm forcefully. Sonia gasped, fearing that the unsuspecting gentleman was about to be attacked. Instead, he looked at the homeless man in shock, and then said, "Mark? Is that you? I don't believe it!"

The two men embraced and started crying. They were only a few feet away from Sonia's table, so she could hear their entire conversation.

The well-dressed man spoke again, "Oh my God, bro, I haven't seen you since 'Nam! What the hell *happened* to you?"

The homeless man shook his head. Suddenly sounding very meek and apologetic, he answered, "I didn't do so well after we returned. I had a really bad case of PTSD, and I haven't been able to get on my feet. It's been really hard."

The well-dressed man then grabbed the wretched, filthy man and gave him the warmest, most heartfelt hug she'd ever seen two men share. "I'm so sorry this happened to you. You're such a good guy. This is unbe-lievable. I can't stand to see you this way." He then took out his wallet and emptied it of all the cash, and shoved it into his old friend's hand. "Here, take this for now," he insisted. "And here's my card. Call me tomorrow, and I promise I'll help you get back on your feet."

They hugged once more for a really long time, and then the well-dressed guy said, "Call me! I mean it. Call me." Then he continued on his way, shaking his head, as if he couldn't believe what had just happened.

The homeless guy stood still for a moment and then put the money in his pocket. He turned around and walked right up to Sonia, and asked, "Do you believe in God?"

Stunned by the interaction that had just taken place and surprised by his question, she hesitated for a second, but then said, "Yes, I do."

"Do you believe in miracles?"

Still absorbing what she'd just witnessed, she an-swered once again, "Yes, I do."

"Well, you just caused a miracle to happen to me. If you hadn't asked me to sit down and order some food, I never would have run into my friend. You just saved my life."

Just then his meal came out. The waiter served it to him as if he were one of the restaurant's most-valued customers and not the ranting lunatic he appeared to be only moments earlier.

Sonia returned to her own meal with Mary, both si-lent with eyes wide open and staring at each other.

The man wolfed down his food in seconds, then got up and approached their table once more.

"Thank you," he said. "Thank you so much." He turned and quietly walked away.

Sonia looked at Mary and said, "I guess that's why we had to stop what we were doing and come here for dinner. We had to help this guy out, and we didn't know it."

"You're absolutely right," Mary agreed. "Seeing what he's been dealing with, I guess we really have nothing to worry about, do we? We're so lucky not to suffer the way he does."

"That's true. We really are."

Still processing the strange unfolding of events, Sonia suddenly blurted out, as if speaking to her own uncertain future, "Things surprisingly work out, so why worry? And we have everything to do with the fact that things can and do work out if we're willing to help each other."

When it was time to leave and the girls asked for the check, their waiter told them that there wasn't one. Their dinner, as well as the homeless man's, was on the house. He paid for them. The night was a gift all the way around.

Making the Shift

The final step in our transformation and living in blessed flow is that of empathy, of responding to life with compassion and a willingness to help other people every single day. As Divine beings, we instinctively recognize that we are all interconnected in such a sublime way that our egos alone can't fully grasp it. We are never really isolated or disconnected from others, other than in our own minds, and as soon as we remember and act on that wisdom, all doors that appear closed, all avenues that seem shut off, suddenly open up.

We move in the highest form of flow when our hearts are the force that moves us. When we stop judging, overthinking, worrying, and separating ourselves from others and from God, and simply follow our natural design to love without hesitation or fear, life becomes a blessed symphony of miracles. As Mother Teresa, the great miracle worker of our time, and one of the most Divinely transformed human beings to walk this earth, once said, "We cannot do great things. We can only do small things with great love."

The choice to do small things with great love is the most fundamentally transforming of all. It is only this that ensures that our shift into Divine consciousness is complete. It is the final awareness we must embrace before we can fully engage the power of our Spirit, and the only information our egos need to learn and practice. To live each day filled with love for life and for our fellow humans, and to express our love through small and consistent acts of compassion, both toward ourselves and others, marks our truest graduation into a completely Divine state of being. The ego would like us to believe that it's far more difficult and complicated than this. It is not. Love is all there is to know, to live, and to share.

Asking the Questions

Now take out your journal and turn your attention inward. Contemplate each of the following questions, and invite your Spirit, your most authentic self, to respond to each one. Give yourself plenty of time to feel the genuine response coming from your heart, the source of your power.

- In what ways could you be more loving and compassionate toward yourself? Are you often overly self-critical? Do you consider yourself unworthy?

- In what ways do you judge others? By their looks? By their lack of accomplishments or status? Whether or not they are educated? By their seeming weaknesses or vulnerabilities? Are these the same things you judge and criticize in yourself?

- When you're around weak or vulnerable people, how do you generally behave? Are you inclined to offer your help or do you tend to look away?

- When it comes to intuition, do you follow your instincts and act, even when your rational mind fights you?

- Can you spontaneously allow yourself to depart from set plans and go with new influences or impulses, or do you always stick to the plan and resist spontaneous diversions?

- Do you genuinely feel a spiritual connection between yourself and others? Does sharing with people you know or even with strangers come easily to you?

- When was the last time you spontaneously experienced the flow of goodness toward you? How did it come about?

- When was the last time you expressed the flow of goodness toward another person? What were you doing? How did you feel afterward?

- How does being in the flow of compassionate love feel when it does occur? Familiar? Secure? Surprising? Tentative? Natural?

After writing down your answers, set aside your journal and remain seated. Close your eyes, and calmly breathe in and out through your nose. Start with a sigh or two to help you relax. Recall a kindness you did for someone. Focus on the way you felt during and afterward. Hold on to the feeling of openness and unconditional love in your heart.

With your next breath, let all of your tension go and simply *be* for a moment or two, even longer if possible. Enjoy sitting and breathing deeply, empty of all thought, free of any agenda, and in the moment. Feel this vibration of being connected to Source. Notice how peaceful, content, and even energized you feel. This is the power of your Spirit, and it's available to you at all times. It is the real you. *Remember this.*

Daily Practice: Cultivate Compassion

Be compassionate. The definition of the word is "a deep awareness of the suffering of another coupled with the wish to relieve it." This doesn't mean that you're supposed to come to the rescue of every troubled soul you meet. It simply invites you to treat those in need with dignity, kindness, patience, and generosity to the best of your ability. People in need cross your path so that you can practice living as a Divine conscious being. The benefit of your loving-kindness is yours to keep. For all you know, those you help may be angels in disguise, eagerly assisting in advancing your education as a fully transformed spiritual being.

Graduate once and for all from the limitations of the ego and establish the deepest possible connection to your kefi—your loving, powerful Spirit—by choosing to live compassionately every day.

> *"If you want others to be happy practice compassion; and if you want yourself to be happy practice compassion."*
>
> — THE DALAI LAMA

When you have setbacks, lose patience, judge, or criticize others, notice how unhappy you feel, how "unwhole" and isolated. Then forgive yourself and start over. Do not exclude yourself from the circle of love and compassion for all of life.

As you're journeying through the stages of transformation, remember that you are an integral part of the circle. Breathe in compassion, breathe out compassion. Breathe in love, breathe out love. Breathe in as Spirit, breathe out as Spirit. Enjoy the benefits, and feel your own unlimited Divine power.

AFTERWORD

The New Frontier

"Teach this triple truth to all: A generous heart, kind speech, and a life of service and compassion are the things which renew humanity."

— THE BUDDHA

Moving through the four stages of transformation as we come to embrace the authentic power of our Spirit is a dynamic and challenging process. Each phase demands our full attention, evokes our worst fears, challenges our limited beliefs, and demands relentless courage, as we're asked to grow in ways that aren't always comfortable or easy.

As we leave the false security of the ego and move back into a true relationship with the Universe as Divine spiritual beings, we often feel as if we're stepping into the abyss and being led into oblivion. In letting go of the old ways of the ego, we die a little with each step we take toward our Spirit. This death—although a welcome liberation from the prison of our own making—can nonetheless be frightening.

Reaching the last stage of transformation and falling into the flow of Divine Spirit is not an ending; rather, it's a wonderful new beginning. As soon as we surrender in love and compassion to the Holy Spirit within, we find ourselves at the threshold of a deeper awakening, followed by a profound degree of discovery. As we further surrender our carefully crafted identities, we'll experience even more magnificent experiences of flow.

The process of Divine expansion and the journey back to Spirit never ends. Not even with death. It just repeats at higher levels of consciousness, an endless spiral of increasing light as we grow brighter—vibrating at increasingly higher frequencies of consciousness and merging into the one power of pure Spirit, pure love.

The question "Will it ever end?" is one we'll never have an absolute answer to as long as we are in human form. We can only continue to transform our ego, follow our light, and remember to live the power of our Spirit through daily practice.

Trust that your journey back to your most authentic self, to the holiest expression of your Spirit, will be successful. Know that absolute freedom from victimhood is ensured if you're faithful in your daily devotion. Little steps are all that we, as humans, can make. Yet each step—in the form of the simple daily practices shared throughout this book—will bring you closer to the great light of love, which is your kefi, your Spirit.

The hour of transformation from limited victim of fearful ego to empowered light being of Spirit is now. The Universe is demanding that you evolve, for your light can no longer be trapped in the darkness of your false self. You're destined to remember who you are and live as you were designed to be: as an empowered, creative, joyful, confident, loving spiritual being, filled with the dance of light, the laughter and play of your Spirit, and the endless love and compassion that is your true nature.

You are not alone—you never were. You are supported at all times and in all ways by unseen holy forces of love that you cannot even begin to imagine. You are connected to all of humanity and to the heart of God. Although you may feel afraid, there is nothing to fear. You are safe. There is no enemy to fight, no struggle to undertake. There are only the dark and threatening walls of your own confusion to dismantle. Relax and surrender. Beyond these artificial barriers lie peace and the greatest of all powers: the fearless power to love.

Slowly and happily all of humankind is learning to flow. Continue to reclaim the joy and power of your Spirit by maintaining a faithful practice. Devote yourself to it. Make tuning in to your authentic self, which is love, the most important thing in your life . . . and your peaceful transformation is ensured.

May your journey through the four stages be blessed and Divine, and may you live in the power of your Spirit forever.

As always, all my love,

THE DAILY
PRACTICES OF
A TRANSFORMED
SPIRITUAL BEING

On a beautiful piece of paper, such as parchment or your favorite stationery, write down the statements on the following pages, and place the sheet on your altar. Alternatively, you can simply photocopy the pages. Every morning when you visit your altar, reach for this paper and read the statements out loud, slowly and clearly.

Sit silently and contemplate these intentions for a few moments. Acknowledge that by living them, you allow the power of your Spirit to lead your life. Focus your attention specifically on where your behavior is not presently aligned with these intentions and resolve to change them one at a time.

Next, gently return the paper back to your altar. Reading these statements out loud on a regular basis will deeply imprint them into your subconscious mind, where they will start to integrate as new patterns of behavior at the deepest level of your awareness. Soon you will memorize them and naturally begin to shape your life choices and responses around them. Eventually, you'll no longer need to think about making these Spirit-based choices; they'll come to you automatically. As the old saying goes, "If you name it, you claim it."

Claim your authentic Divine self with these intentions, and commit to allowing your Spirit to become the leader of your life each and every day from now on. The more you work on it, the more empowered and peaceful you will feel.

As an empowered, transformed spiritual being, I choose to . . .

- Live for the moment.
- Be open to the Holy Spirit dwelling in me.
- Breathe in Spirit before I think, speak, or act.
- Acknowledge the Divine Spirit in all living beings.
- Consciously remember to breathe.
- Actively become aware of and peel away my limiting ego patterns.
- Easily release what no longer serves a useful purpose in my life.
- Silently observe Spirit each day.
- Make choices that are aligned with my authentic self.

- Speak my heart's truth with love.
- Keep the fire of my Spirit burning.
- Do something I love every day.
- Surrender into the flow.
- Accept the ebb.
- Set my intentions, and follow my inspirations daily.
- Pray for guidance.
- Be compassionate toward all beings, including myself.
- Show gratitude for everything in life.
- Enjoy the gift of my life.
- Let my Spirit lead.

ABOUT THE AUTHOR

Sonia Choquette is a world-renowned author, story-teller, vibrational healer, and six-sensory spiritual teacher in international demand for her guidance, wisdom, and capacity to heal the soul. She's the author of several best-selling books, including *The New York Times* best-seller *The Answer Is Simple . . .*, *Ask Your Guides*, *Trust Your Vibes*, and *Soul Lessons and Soul Purpose;* and numerous audio programs and card decks.

Sonia was educated at the University of Denver and the Sorbonne in Paris, and holds a Ph.D. in metaphysics from the American Institute of Holistic Theology. She resides with her family in Chicago.

Website: **www.soniachoquette.com**

HAY HOUSE TITLES OF RELATED INTEREST

YOU CAN HEAL YOUR LIFE, the movie,
starring Louise L. Hay & Friends
(available as an online streaming video)
www.hayhouse.com/louise-movie

THE SHIFT, the movie,
starring Dr. Wayne W. Dyer
(available as an online streaming video)
www.hayhouse.com/the-shift-movie

◎ ◎

EXPERIENCE YOUR GOOD NOW!
Learning to Use Affirmations, by Louise L. Hay

INSIDE-OUT HEALING: Transforming Your Life Through
the Power of Presence, by Richard Moss

INSPIRED DESTINY: Living a Fulfilling
and Purposeful Life, by Dr. John F. Demartini

THE MAP: Finding the Magic and Meaning
in the Story of Your Life, by Colette Baron-Reid

POWER OF THE SOUL: Inside Wisdom
for an Outside World, by John Holland

SOUL COACHING: 28 Days to Discover
Your Authentic Self, by Denise Linn

TIME FOR TRUTH: A New Beginning, by Nick Bunick

TRANSFORMING FATE INTO DESTINY:
A New Dialogue with Your Soul, by Robert Ohotto

All of the above are available at your local bookstore,
or may be ordered by contacting Hay House (see next page).

◎ ◎

We hope you enjoyed this Hay House book. If you'd like to receive our online catalog featuring additional information on Hay House books and products, or if you'd like to find out more about the Hay Foundation, please contact:

Hay House, Inc., P.O. Box 5100, Carlsbad, CA 92018-5100
(760) 431-7695 or (800) 654-5126
(760) 431-6948 (fax) or (800) 650-5115 (fax)
www.hayhouse.com® • www.hayfoundation.org

———

Published in Australia by: Hay House Australia Pty. Ltd.,
18/36 Ralph St., Alexandria NSW 2015
Phone: 612-9669-4299 • *Fax:* 612-9669-4144
www.hayhouse.com.au

Published in the United Kingdom by: Hay House UK, Ltd.,
The Sixth Floor, Watson House, 54 Baker Street, London W1U 7BU
Phone: +44 (0)20 3927 7290 • *Fax:* +44 (0)20 3927 7291
www.hayhouse.co.uk

Published in India by: Hay House Publishers India,
Muskaan Complex, Plot No. 3, B-2, Vasant Kunj, New Delhi 110 070
Phone: 91-11-4176-1620 • *Fax:* 91-11-4176-1630
www.hayhouse.co.in

———

<u>Access New Knowledge.</u>
<u>Anytime. Anywhere.</u>

Learn and evolve at your own pace
with the world's leading experts.

www.hayhouseU.com